10221455

D1549263

■ Structuring Dran

A Handbook of Available Forms in Theatre and Drama

Jonothan Neelands

Edited by Tony Goode

With a Foreword by Professor David Booth

■

CAMBRIDGE
UNIVERSITY PRESS

Acknowledgements   This book has gone through a long period of gestation. The idea of identifying dramatic conventions occurred some time ago, but the need for the classification system used in the book, together with the notes on structuring, have only recently emerged as a result of working with many teachers and youth theatre workers from all phases of education over the last two years. During this time, Paul Bunyan, Jo Boulton, Lesley Lyon and Geoff Readman have had a profound influence on my thinking about theatre.

I would also like to acknowledge other groups of people whose work I have been privileged to share, and whose practice has clarified the notes on structuring:

Teachers involved in the Leicester Mode 3 GCSE in Northamptonshire, Nottinghamshire and Cambridgeshire;

The Dukes Playhouse Theatre-in-Education Company from Lancaster who taught me so much about theatre during my time as education officer to the company;

Teachers from Ontario whom I have worked with in Toronto and London over several years—particularly David Booth who is opening up new ways of seeing educational theatre for me;

Chris Hughes for his work on clarifying and producing the diagrams in the book.

Finally, I would like to thank Tony Goode not just for his role as editor, but also for the many ideas he has contributed to the book, as well as for the hours of patient discussion which helped to form the complex ideas and the classification system underpinning the book.

PUBLISHED BY THE PRESS SYNDICATE OF THE UNIVERSITY OF CAMBRIDGE
The Pitt Building, Trumpington Street, Cambridge CB2 1RP, United Kingdom

CAMBRIDGE UNIVERSITY PRESS
The Edinburgh Building, Cambridge CB2 2RU, United Kingdom
40 West 20th Street, New York, NY 10011−4211, USA
10 Stamford Road, Oakleigh, Melbourne 3166, Australia

© Cambridge University Press 1990

First published 1990
Ninth printing 1997

Printed in the United Kingdom at the University Press, Cambridge

A catalogue record for this book is available from the British Library

ISBN 0 521 37635 1

■ Contents

■ Foreword

Each summer for the last five years, the University of Toronto has run, with Jonothan Neelands and Tony Goode, an extension campus in London for teachers enrolled in a Specialist Programme in Drama. The courses have been an enormous success. I have worked with both Tony and Jonothan in North America several times as well, and the professional relationship and the personal friendship that has grown from these collaborations strengthens my life and my work.

These connections that are found among countries can only strengthen the role of drama as a power in educating young people. The hundreds of teachers who have travelled in England, those in North America who have been part of the courses, workshops and seminars are now part of a large network of people who are struggling to understand and use this world of theatre as a means of helping young people to grow. I hope the tradition of exchange will continue to help teachers develop as drama educators.

Both Jonothan and Tony base their work in theatre, and the teachers who participate in their classes are freed from dichotomies and controversies that have plagued us for such a long time. Of course their definition of theatre is much more inclusive than those traditionally argued. They see theatre as the 'direct experience shared when people imagine and behave as if they were other than themselves in some other place and at another time'. It is a meaning-making endeavour that interprets life and helps us to understand our world. Like other art forms, it uses symbols as a means of shaping and crafting and expressing feelings and ideas, and participants are involved both as spectator and participant, in exploration and in performance.

The conventions that Jonothan Neelands sets out for us to use as teachers give us techniques to work with in helping young people both to learn through theatre experiences and to learn about theatre by controlling the medium. These conventions allow us to work alongside our students in exploring content and form, learning about each from working and reflecting inside the experience. In addition, the second half of this book places this 'palette of conventions' inside frames that give teachers the processes and structures necessary for making drama happen.

The teachers from North America who have worked through this schema of theatre conventions now understand the elements that make up drama lessons, but more important, they have seen the two skilled British educators demonstrate the craft and sensitivity that are prerequisites for growth in theatre arts. Drama in schools and youth theatres only occurs when students experience the content and the form together as one and when the art of theatre is felt and understood within the context of the work being explored. The teachers who took part in the sessions will testify that these two educators can both create moments of drama and also help them to reflect upon and understand *how* it happened, and how to set about to make it happen again.

Helping teachers to make drama happen within the theatre mode has been the goal of many courses, books, articles and seminars. How to integrate theory and practice, how to believe in the students and the art form, how to structure lessons and units of work – these are the quests of drama teachers.

In reading this book, I am made aware constantly of the richness of the strategies embedded in it, of the clarity of the manner in which they are presented and of the integrity behind the choice of words and ideas. We begin with play, and we grow into theatre, knowing its power and its purity, and we share as a tribe in this particular art form that is meant for all.

This book is about the aesthetic search that directs the work of drama teachers, and Jonothan and Tony share with us the learnings from their lives as educators. It is much appreciated and it is a book that will go a long way towards healing the drama/theatre rift.

David Booth
University of Toronto

■ Introduction

The purpose of this book is to outline some of the conventions that are available to teachers/leaders and students in structuring dramatic activity; whether it be an improvised workshop, an active exploration of a text and its meanings, or a participatory workshop for other students. In addition, the book sets out models for the process of structuring dramatic activity so that the use of conventions can be seen as part of a dynamic process which enables students to make, explore and communicate meaning through theatre form.

The book is not an exhaustive guide to the practical study of theatre; rather, it identifies varieties of form that might be used or experienced as part of the more comprehensive art-process of communicating and interpreting meanings through theatre.

It is assumed that, as with all art-forms, the experience of theatre is distinguished from real-life experience by the conscious application of form to meaning in order to engage both the intellect and the emotions in a representation of meaning. In theatre, meanings, social codes and interactions are represented, shaped and crafted through the conventions of dramatic activity. The same would hold true for all other art-forms which use recognizable and conscious conventions of form in order to convey meanings. It is assumed that understanding the possibilities (and limitations) of form gives insight into the medium of theatre, and offers students the possibility of operating greater control over the medium and its personal and social uses.

■ Definitions of theatre and dramatic convention

The definitions of theatre and dramatic convention presented below assume the following:

☐ that the term theatre does not describe a single form of activity e.g. the performance of a playwright's work to an audience;

☐ that theatre exists as a process for the interpretation of human behaviour and meanings as well as for their expression; it responds to a basic human need to symbolize the world through art-forms;

☐ that meaningful and personally useful theatre activity is the right and prerogative of all people, enabling all to maximize the culture of their race, class, gender, age or ability;

☐ that a comprehensive study of theatre needs to go beyond a consideration of dramatic texts and skills associated with acting;

☐ that understanding theatre is an active process that enables a student to build from subjective responses to theatre experiences towards the formation of valid critical judgements and generalizations about the nature and availability of theatre.

For the purposes of this book the following working definitions are used:

Theatre is the direct experience that is shared when people imagine and behave as if they were other than themselves in some other place at another time. This definition seeks to encompass all forms of creative imitative behaviour—from the loose and spontaneous imaginative *play* of young children (which becomes internalized, but still used in later life as a way of rehearsing conversations and events to come) through to the more formal experience of *the play* performed by actors for an audience.

Meanings in theatre are created for both spectator and participant through the actor's fictional and symbolic uses of human presence in time and space. These may be enhanced by the symbolic use of objects, light and sound. Dramatic convention describes the form that this relationship takes at different stages of the theatrical experience.

Conventions are indicators of the way in which *time, space* and *presence* can interact and be imaginatively shaped to create different kinds of meanings in theatre. Different conventions will, therefore, emphasize different qualities in the theatrical possibilities of time, space and human presence. In terms of time, for instance, an improvisation will create a relationship that is very close to reality in the sense that time elapses at life-rate and the actor behaves and uses space naturalistically; in **Still-image** time is arrested and frozen so that a period of time can be spent inquiring into a single moment represented in the tableau; in **Mimed activity** the actor's use of space is often overtly symbolic, going beyond 'natural' gesture and uses of space in order to communicate specific meanings.

Part One of this book provides some of the conventions that make up the 'palette' that teachers/leaders and students use in theatre; the application of the palette to create a picture requires those skills of sensitivity, perception and craft which develop through practical involvement and experimentation in theatre itself. Parts Two and Three, therefore, introduce processes which may assist students and teachers/leaders in exploring the applications of the palette of conventions.

Part 1 A Guide to Dramatic Conventions

■ Rationale

The definitions of theatre offered above have stressed a broad unity across a range of activities which have the imaginative and fictional use of time, space, and presence as their common feature. Theatre is not seen as a narrow or exclusive set of culturally bound forms. The definitions are chosen in order to fix the book in contexts where theatre is being created by young people and in recognition of the need to define a process in theatre which provides a continuity and development of experience across an age range that finds its first theatre experiences in play; to a generation which finds its satisfaction in a wide variety of contexts, including seeing and being in plays. The definitions influenced the selection of conventions in two important ways which, together, reflect the values of theatre and education held in this book:

☐ The conventions and the examples emphasize interactive forms of interchange, even fusion, of the roles of spectator and actor, rather than those conventions associated with performance where the roles of spectator and actor tend to be more clearly defined. *The conventions selected are mainly concerned with the process of theatre as a means of developing understanding about both human experience and theatre itself.* This may, or may not, later become translated and communicated through performance.

☐ The conventions have been chosen to emphasize theatre's traditional role as an educative form of entertainment which responds to a basic human need to interpret and express the world through symbolic form. The conventions recognize that theatre is not taught, rather that our own basic uses of theatre in play and other forms of imitative behaviour become refined and developed by experiencing increasingly complex relationships of convention and content. *The conventions selected, therefore, form a bridge between spontaneous and innate uses of theatre and the more poetic conventions of performance craft.* They are consciously associated with other familiar youth culture forms in order to stress the familiarity and pervasiveness of theatre.

■ Classification and Criteria for Selection

The conventions have been organized into groups which represent four varieties of dramatic action:

5 ■

○ **Context-building action**

> Conventions which either 'set the scene', or add information to the context of the drama as it unfolds.

◇ **Narrative action**

> Conventions which tend to emphasize the 'story' or 'what-happens-next' dimension of the drama.

▽ **Poetic action**

> Conventions which emphasize or create the symbolic potential of the drama through highly selective use of language and gesture.

□ **Reflective action**

> Conventions which emphasize 'soliloquy' or 'inner-thinking' in the drama, or allow groups to review the drama from within the dramatic context.

This classification is not intended to be hierarchical or sequential. A convention achieves value through being appropriate to the moment it has been selected for, and the dynamic nature of theatre requires shifts to and from different varieties of action as the experience unfolds.

The idea of a classification system is based on the notion that any such classification will be fluid in its boundaries and serve as a means of making the entire list of conventions more manageable when choices about form need to be taken. The handling of a convention in practice may result in a cross-over of boundaries; a move from narrative action to poetic action, for instance.

The classification has been developed in response to certain basic needs required for participation, either as a spectator or as an actor, in dramatic activity:

□ **Need for a clearly defined context**

> Theatre presents us with imagined situations in which a shared understanding of place, time, characters and other contextual information becomes crucial to the quality of involvement in the experience.

□ **Need to nurture and create an interest in 'what happens next'**

> Theatre is defined as a narrative form, like story and film, in which curiosity about the story line and a sense of imminent action act as motivation for those acting or spectating in the dramatic event.

☐ **Need to recognize and create a symbolic dimension to the work**

Theatre provides a means of looking beyond the immediate story or plot through the symbols, ambiguities and imagery which are capable of crystallizing, projecting and holding the essence of an experience.

☐ **Need to reflect on the meanings and themes which emerge through the experience**

Theatre provides a 'mirror' for actors and spectators to consider themselves and their relationship to others.

☐ **Need for choices to be made about the form of the work**

Emphasis on students' gaining knowledge of the demands and uses of different conventions allows for a negotiated choice of conventions. *Psychologically, the group need to feel comfortable and protected enough to risk themselves in the convention. The teacher/leader or facilitator often needs to negotiate a convention which creates a balance between the desire to motivate and inspire the group and the need to keep the activity controlled and manageable.*

■ Organization of Entries for the Conventions

The entry for each convention is necessarily brief and practically orientated. An entry does not aim to represent a convention fully in its complexity. Indeed, an understanding of the particularity or essential qualities of a convention is seen as growing, in part, from the students' active experimentation with form. It develops also through a shared analysis of the interaction between form and content which begins when the students are provided with the opportunity and climate in which to articulate and make sense of their own felt-responses to the use of a convention in practice.

The entry for each convention is arranged under the following headings:

■ Description

An explanation of how the convention is operated, and the different forms it might take. There will be many other variations of each convention which are not identified.

■ Cultural connections

The purpose of this section is to recognize and raise the status of theatre as a cultural resource that taps young people's shared understanding of media/story conventions as well as conventions associated with their own immediate culture—which in turn reflects specific class, gender and racial variations and qualities. There is an emphasis on conventions that are borrowed from, or closely connect with, popular culture.

■ Learning opportunity

Each convention mediates and transforms meanings in a different way. For instance, meanings associated with family life are fundamentally different when expressed through dance conventions as opposed to monologue or soliloquy. This heading attempts to give a broad outline of the learning features highlighted by each convention in order to give some idea of what each represents as a form of learning.

■ Examples

Very brisk snapshots of conventions in practice which illustrate a convention being used for a particular purpose. The examples are not complete lessons or workshops; they are isolated moments taken from more extensive and coherent programmes.

Two of the major limitations of this section need to be stressed:

☐ Within the section each convention described appears isolated from others by the need to identify and separate conventions for the sake of clarity. In practice there is an integration of form in which conventions run into each other, or overlap, or merge into new composite conventions. An essential feature of theatre is that the dramatic experience develops and accumulates so that responses to a convention used at one stage in the experience have to be taken within the context of the responses generated by the previous convention and the responses offered by the convention that follows. The possibility of creating relationships between conventions in order to develop ideas or to give an appropriate rhythm to the structure of a dramatic exercise is seen as a central skill-area in theatre;

☐ The list of conventions which follows is not intended to impress or overwhelm in terms of quantity: *the real skill is not in making lists but in knowing which convention to select in order to establish appropriateness between:*

(a) the needs and experience of the group;
(b) the content chosen for the drama;
(c) opportunities for learning.

A. Context-Building Action $\bigcirc$

Soundtracking	Unfinished Materials
Role-on-the-wall	Diaries, Letters, Journals, Messages
Costuming	Making Maps/Diagrams
Defining Space	Still-Image
Collective Drawing	Simulations
Games	

Uses

These conventions enable a group to create or engage with the dramatic context: the concrete particulars of the situation, characters or roles which will inform and drive the action. They are helpful when there is a need to:

☐ clarify the context through fixing time, place, people involved;

☐ create atmosphere through use of space, light, sound;

☐ draw attention to contextual constraints or opportunities;

☐ find and make symbols and themes for the work;

☐ check out possibly different interpretations of the context held in the group.

Cultural origins

Life experience of building dens, designing rooms, arranging furniture; expectations created by different settings—dark woods, high-tech rooms, etc. Conventions are drawn from theatre/film e.g. set-building, costuming and from psychotherapy e.g. games, simulations and still-image.

Level of demand

Because the work is to do with setting up the context, rather than acting within it, there is little threat or personal risk involved. The work is indirect and involves groups contributing to a context which will be shared. *Commitment to dramatic action is gained through the small group work and the sense of ownership generated, as well as through the interest created in seeing how the context might be used in the drama.*

○ Soundtracking

Description	Realistic or stylized sounds accompany action, or describe an environment. Dialogue is devised to fit a given piece of action. Sound from one situation is 'dubbed' onto another. Voices or instruments are used to create a mood or paint a picture.
Cultural connections	Sound effects on film and TV; street sounds; pop videos; music on film and TV; noises that disturb—being followed, breaking glass, etc.
Learning opportunities	Matching sound to action; using sound poetically and expressively to convey mood and a sense of place; exploring dissonance between soundtrack and images; encouraging confidence in voice as a wide-ranging instrument.

Examples **1.** A group is working on the 'Great Fire of London'. As Museum curators they reconstruct Pudding Lane, using blocks, chairs and tables. They represent waxworks in the reconstruction, showing the different trades, home and street activities of the time. A switch is pushed which starts a soundtrack of the sounds of the street. The sound starts at one end of the lane and travels down, adding new sounds as it goes. Later, the fire moves down the lane in much the same way.

2. In order to slow down the pace of a 'robbery' drama whilst sustaining the tension building up to the actual theft, some of the group mime what's going on in the bank as they listen to the robbers making their plans in some other place.

○ Role-on-the-Wall

Description	An important, pivotal role is represented in picture form or diagram 'on the wall'; information is read or added as the drama progresses. Individuals may take it in turns to adopt the role in improvisations, so that it becomes a collective representation rather than a personal interpretation.
Cultural connections	Portraits; posters; characters in books, films, TV; legendary figures; caricatures; cartoons; personal records and files; imitating, mimicking well-known figures.
Learning opportunities	Distanced, reflective way of building a deep understanding of a role; building a complex character from scratch; sharing a role through alternative portrayals; strong form for exploring human characteristics and behaviour.

Examples **1.** As a means of exploring the experience of old age, the group are shown a highly selective, atmospheric, life-size charcoal and chalk drawing of an old man with a series of factual statements about his life. The drawings and statements contain a rich variety of signs about the old man's likely attitudes to old age. As a way into the work, the group recreate the man's life in the manner of a photo album.

2. In a drama looking at the story of a disturbed teenager, the teacher draws a rough outline of a human figure. As a starting point, the group add a series of statements made about the figure by a parent, a teacher, a psychologist, and a friend; these are written beside the figure. As the work progresses, new understandings about the teenager are written inside the figure as an aid to reflection and to record the growing complexity of the characterization.

○ Costuming

Description	Articles of costume or significant cultural objects are presented as an introduction to a culture or a lifestyle or a character; or decisions are taken about what costume it would be appropriate to introduce during the drama; or individuals use costume to help build belief in their role.
Cultural connections	Fancy dress; dressing up—special occasions, discos, 'going out'; make-up; fashions; styles; uniforms; making clothes; clothes worn for jobs; clothes that other generations wear.
Learning opportunities	Matching costumes to character; reflecting on artefacts, clothing as symbols for cultural beliefs and attitudes; creating characters from cultural clues; deepening understanding of cultural differences; reflecting on clothing as an expression of identity.

Examples **1.** The teacher asks the group to establish a character from a bundle of clothes and belongings that have been found on a cliff. The bundle includes an old jacket, baggy trousers, muddy rag bandages, a length of string, a knife, a woollen cap, a bundle of newspapers, a tobacco tin, a rag doll, a tripod and cooking tin. From these clues, the group create the role of Albert, a derelict traveller, and they go on to discuss what each object reveals about the man who owns them. The subsequent drama is to do with discovering what might have happened to Albert.

2. A peace pipe is presented to a group working on a Native American project. In order to explore its significance, the group consider it from a range of imagined viewpoints:

☐ as archæologists who have found the pipe and are speculating on its use;

☐ as historians arranging the best way of presenting the pipe in a museum display;

☐ as present-day Indians reflecting on their 'lost culture'.

◯ Defining Space

Description	Available material and furniture is used to 'accurately' represent the place where a drama is happening; or to represent the physical scale of something in the drama; or to fix the position and proximity of rooms, houses, places where events have taken place.
Cultural connections	Sets used in media drama; film locations; re-arranging furniture of home; imaginative use of adventure playgrounds and other 'hanging-about' places.
Learning opportunities	Using available resources imaginatively; negotiating the way a place should look; representing meanings spatially: encouraging belief in the fiction by working to elaborate it; reflecting on relationships between context and action.

Examples

1. As a way in to considering the effect of imprisonment on women, groups working as architects are asked to build cells using available materials, so that the dimensions and what is inside the cell can be seen. The 'cells' are compared and discussed, and then compared against the dimensions of an actual cell and against regulations covering what is allowed inside.

2. The group are at an inquiry into the murder of a young film star on a film set. The group reconstruct the film set using available materials, and position the body as it would have looked when it was first discovered.

○ Collective Drawing

Description	The class or small groups make a collective image to represent a place or people in the drama. The image then becomes a concrete reference for ideas that are being discussed, or which are half-perceived.
Cultural connections	Illustrations; media imagery; photos of urban/rural landscapes; portraits; use of drawing for own purposes; comics; cartoons; posters; postcards.
Learning opportunities	Giving form to imagined places and faces; negotiating a common response in relation to appearances; researching authenticity in drawings of alien cultures or historical periods; division of labour in performing the task.

Examples **1.** A group of 'pioneers' are planning to go West on a wagon-train. In order to establish their motives for undertaking such an epic journey, and how it fits with their past, the group prepare two collective drawings for display—one represents the place they have migrated from, with clues as to what made them leave; the second represents their imaginings of their eventual destination.

2. A group working on 'Mining' have just read Sid Chaplin's *Hands* (Penguin English Project 'Danger', Ward Lock). The story describes an accident in which the narrator's father is crushed by a fall, so that his hands are left exposed. In the role of book illustrators, groups work with charcoal and chalk to make a representative image showing the end of the story.

◯ Games

Description	Traditional games, or variations, are used to establish trust, confidence or to establish rules; games are selected to simplify a complex experience; games are put into the context of drama rather than played for their own sake.
Cultural connections	Street games; quiz shows; card, board games, team games; psychological games; computer games; educational games; tests of skill, strength, endurance.
Learning opportunities	Highly controlled, players must submit to rules; enjoyable, fun activity; highlights tensions in social situations; useful for breaking the ice, getting to know people; reveals game structures in life situations—blocking, hiding, deceiving, etc.

Examples

1. As part of their work on World War I, a group participate in a number of training games in preparation for going to the Front. One game is a variation of 'Lifeboats/Captain's coming' where the recruits have to respond instantly to various commands:

'Captain's coming'—stand to attention, salute;
'Shells'   —drop flat on the floor;
'Bayonets'   —push a bayonet into an enemy and twist;
'Digging'   —dig frantically with spade.

The game reveals the inadequacy of training, the need for alert, quick responses, the ruthless authoritarianism of trainers and the idea of combat as game.

2. In a murder inquiry, a number of suspects have been identified. In order to conclude the drama, the suspects secretly draw lots to see who the killer is. The rest of the group then interrogate suspects, looking for evidence of guilt. They decide who they think the murderer is and why; the murderer then reveals herself and gives her motive for the crime.

○ Unfinished Materials

Description	An object, article of clothing, newspaper cutting, letter, or opening to a story is introduced as a starting point for the development of a drama. The participants build on the clues and partial information offered in order to construct a drama to explore and develop themes, events and meanings suggested by the unfinished materials.
Cultural connections	Trailers for film and TV; adventure stories; lyrics; speculations on events behind the news; maps; diaries; using primary evidence in history; documentaries.
Learning opportunities	Encourages speculation, construction of narrative, collection of evidence; gives participants ownership over the development of the material by providing choices and the opportunity for the group's hypotheses to be worked through dramatically; requires detailed and extensive inter-personal negotiation and a collective approach to meaning-making.

Examples

1. As an introduction to work focusing on the experiences of children moved from children's homes to Australia in the forties and fifties, students are shown an authentic advertisement placed by an English social worker in an Australian newspaper. The advertisement asks for adults who were sent as orphaned children to Australia to contact the social worker with information about their experiences. The group use the advertisement as a starting point for imagining the roles of people who might respond to it and for devising scenes representing some of the experiences they might want to share with the social worker.

2. A fourth-year class are introduced to *Romeo and Juliet* by a group of older students who show a series of tableaux from the play. The fourth-years are given the lines which the tableaux illustrate and asked which figures they belong to. They then create scenes to link the tableaux before looking at the whole play.

○ Diaries, Letters, Journals, Messages

Description	These are written in or out of role as a means of reflecting on experience; or introduced into the drama by the teacher as a new tension, or as evidence; or they are used as a means of reviewing work or building up a cumulative account of a long sequence of work.
Cultural connections	Personal diaries; books and stories written in journal or diary form; ansaphones; telegrams; letters from relatives and friends; letters to the press; secret codes; cryptic messages; spy stories; travelogues.
Learning opportunities	Selecting content; adopting appropriate registers and vocabulary; writing from alternative viewpoints; arousing curiosity with unexpected or cryptic messages; providing a form for reflection; motivating purposes for writing; providing imagined audiences for writing.

Examples **1.** In a drama concerned with the effects of prison on different kinds of offenders, the teacher takes the role of various prisoners each of whom reacts differently to solitary confinement. So that the group can observe each 'prisoner's' behaviour and gain some insight into their background, the teacher is in the cell writing a letter. As she writes, the group hear the words she is actually writing down and also hear her thinking about the words she is choosing, the person she is writing to and what she is thinking but does not write down.

2. In constructing a context for a murder inquiry, a group work on providing some of the clues found at the scene of the crime e.g. still-images representing photos found in the victim's bag. The teacher suggests that the victim was clutching the fragments of a letter when found. Each small group makes two fragments with a word on each; these are then arranged on a grid to see if they give a clue to what the original message might have been.

○ Making Maps/Diagrams

Description	Making maps/diagrams is used as part of the drama in order to reflect on experience e.g. obstacles to be overcome, distance to travel; or to aid problem-solving e.g. 'what's the best way of getting into the bank?'; or after the drama, as a means of reviewing the work; or introduced by the teacher as a stimulus.
Cultural connections	Maps—old and new; making things from instructions/diagrams; giving/receiving directions; treasure/secret maps; map/diagram conventions in thriller/journey stories; map-work in humanities.
Learning opportunities	Getting detail/layout/scale of maps accurate and comprehensible; representing problems diagrammatically; deciphering/interpreting maps and symbols; reflecting on what maps/diagrams tell us about the experience they represent.

Examples **1.** In order to start off an investigative drama into the sale of powdered baby milk in the Third World, the teacher introduces two graphs. The first shows a dramatic decline in sales in UK/USA between 1972–76. The second shows a dramatic increase in Kenyan/Nigerian sales from 1974–80. The group are then put in role as the board of directors and explore the graphs looking at what decisions taken in 1973–74 might have led to the switch of markets.

2. A group of bank robbers gain access to the blueprints of a high-security bank to help them plan their robbery. They represent their route on a transparency that can be laid over the blueprint so that they can explain to other groups the advantages and disadvantages of their plan.

○ Still-Image

Description	Groups devise an image using their own bodies to crystallize a moment, idea or theme; or an individual acts as sculptor to a group. Contrasting images are made to represent actual/ideal, dream/nightmare versions.
Cultural connections	Book illustrations; freeze frame on a video; photographs; portraits; advertisements; sculptures; waxworks' posters; record sleeves; murals.
Learning opportunities	Highly selective way of crystallizing meaning into concrete images, a very economical and controlled form of expression as well as a sign to be interpreted or read by observers; groups are able to represent more than they would be able to communicate through words alone; a useful way of representing 'tricky' content like fights; simplifies complex content into easily managed and understandable form; requires reflection and analysis in the making and observing of images.

Examples 1. A group are working on the theme of 'Runaways' and are at the stage of considering why a young person might want to go to London. Groups devise an image representing the climax of a daydream a young person has about what he/she will become in London e.g. on stage at Wembley, being photographed by David Bailey, knocking out Frank Bruno.

Later in the work the groups devise a contrasting image to illustrate the parents' fears for their child in London after he/she has run away e.g. sleeping rough, being mugged, being tempted with crime/drugs.

2. Groups are in a drama where an urban community is making decisions about development in their area, in particular about how a piece of waste land might be improved for the public good. At a meeting the local council hand round photographs that show how the waste land is currently being used. Groups devise 'photographs' to show how they think the waste land would be used e.g. BMX track, dump for old cars, refuge for homeless and drug addicts, gang headquarters, etc.

○ Simulations

Description	Life events are simulated in such a way as to emphasize management of resources, decision-taking, problem-solving, institutional management. A time limit is often set for 'players', so that there is a game tension. Simulations may be a commercially produced pack including role cards, pretend money and other pieces or a pack produced by one group for another.
Cultural connections	War games; 'Dungeons and Dragons'; Computer games; 'Monopoly'; 'Risk'; etc.
Learning opportunities	Problems presented within contexts that require group decision-making and problem-solving; structured but encourages identification with the problem; rules and prepared materials make it possible for complex interactions between supply and demand, time and personnel to be examined.

Examples

1. As part of a project looking at development and aid strategies, students decide between projects submitted by other groups. They have a fixed budget to allocate and use their own criteria for selection. The exercise involves interviewing proposers and potential beneficiaries of the schemes, and encourages students to look for a balance between cost and long-term effect.

2. Research for a documentary drama on homelessness involves students in a simulation in which they have a set number of places to distribute amongst a group who present themselves as homeless. The students use their local Council's criteria in order to decide who gets the shelter. The drama goes on to explore the consequences for those getting shelter and those who are left homeless.

B. Narrative Action

> Telephone/Radio Conversations
> Mantle of the Expert
> Meetings
> Interviews/Interrogations
> Whole-Group Role-Play
> A Day in the Life
>
> Hot-Seating
> Overheard Conversations
> Reportage
> Noises Off
> Teacher-in-Role

Uses

These conventions are used to focus on significant events, incidents or encounters which will be central to the development of the narrative, or to introduce and develop plot. They allow groups to test out their hypotheses and speculations about the narrative through dramatic involvement; they involve individuals and groups moving the story on through the use of language and behaviour appropriate to the context.

Cultural origins

These are drawn from social conventions found in life, where behaviour is regularized and roles are observed e.g. in meetings, court-rooms, interviews, family rituals, etc. These are characterized by a natural use of time, space, presence, and the experience of the conventions being life-like (the term 'living-through' is sometimes associated with these conventions).

Level of demand

The nature of the conventions is generally recognizable to young people from their own life-experience; the roles of actor and spectator tend to be clear even if they are interchangeable within the convention. Conventions may rely upon there being one or more individuals who are prepared to risk themselves in role. This may depend on them feeling secure that spectators will value their role behaviour. The willingness to enter into action will be influenced by the level of interest and curiosity in the context or story as it unfolds. The naturalness of the conventions makes them a comfortable way of creating theatre for particular groups.

◇ Telephone/Radio Conversations

Description	These may be two-way conversations devised in pairs—to illuminate the present situation, or to break news, or to inform; or a one-way conversation, where the group only hears one side of the conversation. The teacher may use the convention to seek advice, create an outside pressure or introduce new information.
Cultural connections	CB radio jargon; telephone calls—bad news, surprises, conversations with friends or relatives, making excuses, calls for information; listening to others on the telephone; telephone conventions in thrillers/detective stories.
Learning opportunities	Devising appropriate dialogue; adding tension to situation; deciphering/interpreting information; matching register/ vocabulary to purpose of conversation; communicating without relying on gesture.

Examples

1. In a science fiction story a group of victims of persecution have found safe refuge on a new planet and have begun to rebuild their lives in safety and peace. They pick up a faint radio signal from an incoming spaceship. The spaceship comes from their persecutors' planet which has been destroyed by war. The persecutors beg to be allowed to land and ask for forgiveness. What do the victims do?

2. A group of scientists and media people arrive in a remote Scottish community to investigate rumours that a UFO has landed nearby. They are escorted to the police station where the local sergeant feigns ignorance of the matter. She rings her superiors and, in the conversation that follows, there are clues that suggest that the sergeant knows more than she is saying and is part of a conspiracy of silence. Eventually her superiors tell her to make the group sign the Official Secrets Act before she says anything more.

◇ Mantle of the Expert

Description	The group become characters endowed with specialist knowledge that is relevant to the situation: historians, social workers, mountain climbers. The situation is usually task-orientated so that expert understanding or skills are required to perform the task.
Cultural connections	Actual or media experience of teachers, social workers, historians, archivists, designers, builders, architects, carpenters, plumbers, doctors, etc.
Learning opportunities	Power and responsibility move from teacher to group; learners feel respected by having expert status; insights and understanding of different expert occupations are explored; provides distance from experience through professional codes/ethics.

Examples

1. The teacher is in the role of anxious community leader concerned about the number of young drug-takers in her community, and seeks the help of a group of advertisers and educational psychologists. The community leader is concerned that current anti-drug publicity is not really touching young people. The group list all the skills, knowledge and understanding they possess in their expert roles and use these in order to design a campaign that really works. They then go on to produce the campaign.

2. A group working on the theme of 'Looking after elderly people' are invited, as architects, to research their needs. They then design and build a suitable living environment for a group of old people.

◇ Meetings

Description	The group are gathered together within the drama to hear new information, plan action, make collective decisions and suggest strategies to solve problems that have arisen. The meeting may be chaired by the teacher or committee or other individuals—the group may meet without the teacher being present.
Cultural connections	Parliament; form-meetings; assemblies; gang meetings; family discussions; parish council; public inquiries; inquests; hustings; union meetings; picket lines; protest marches.
Learning opportunities	Very structured, with the teacher as Chair having control of proceedings; need to balance individual's needs and interests with other people's; emphasis on negotiation, bargaining, making a case; useful way of calmly considering alternatives and of starting/summarizing a drama.

Examples **1.** As a way of working on the theme of 'School', the group are the school staff and are told about the problems being caused within a particular class. The staff are asked to recount problems that have occurred in their classrooms, and are then asked to suggest and evaluate strategies for dealing with the trouble-makers.

2. Residents of a well-to-do village are brought together to hear the news that a rehabilitation centre is to open in a derelict house in their village. Later, a small group attend a meeting with the shifty owner of the property who is clearly exploiting the prisoners. Another group meet with an ex-prisoner who accuses them of double standards, saying that at least the property owner is offering shelter and work. The villagers meet again to discuss their position.

◇ Interviews/Interrogations

Description	These are challenging, demanding situations designed to reveal information, attitudes, motives, aptitudes and capabilities. One party has the task of eliciting response through appropriate questioning.
Cultural connections	Being in trouble; reporting to parents, teachers, friends; detective stories; court cases; interviews for jobs; orals; news and documentary programmes.
Learning opportunities	Framing appropriate questions and strategies; deciding on what information is required and on whether to trust the responses; sequencing and piecing together of information; gives confidence and develops social skills necessary in real-life situations; contrasts outsider/insider views of events; task-oriented activity.

Examples

1. A class is working on a 'Witchcraft' theme. They have 'built' a village that has a long history of rumours about witchcraft, stretching back to the 16th-century witchcraft trials. The group is split into pairs: in each pair, A is a BBC producer researching for a programme on witchcraft; B is a villager who may, or may not, wish to disclose information about her village and its history. After the interview A reports back to his/her superior at the BBC

2. A group preparing for a drama concerned with development strategies in the Third World are interviewed by VSO as to their skills, aptitudes, attitudes and past relevant experiences, so as to build up a picture of the value of voluntary aid. The group then interview the teacher in the role of various flawed but enthusiastic volunteers, and have to decide on and give their assessment of each.

◇ Whole-Group Role-Play

Description	The whole group (including teacher/leader) behave as if they were an imagined group facing a situation as it actually unfolds around them. Language and behaviour are restricted to the situation and characters involved, so that all negotiations amongst the group must be within, and appropriate to, the symbolic dimension.
Cultural connections	Early experiences of imaginative play; group fantasies; team games; active experience of film or theatre with friends; collective imaginings about how groups might behave or react in different situations.
Learning opportunities	A natural way of working which removes the pressure of being watched by others while working symbolically. The group has to manage problems by reading and contributing to a complex inter-play between the real and symbolic dimensions of their activity. This often serves as an effective means of developing tension and narrative, and as a means of developing personal and group interest in a dramatic context.

Examples **1.** As part of a drama which considers the social effects and consequences of the Alabama bus boycott of 1955, the group assume the roles of civil rights activists involved in a boycott march through Montgomery, Alabama. They encounter the teacher/leader in role as an elderly black woman determined to catch the next bus. The group have to manage the encounter as if it was actually happening to them, which involves discovering and negotiating the limits of the action they are prepared to take in order to secure the success of their boycott.

2. As an introduction to work on Joshua Sobol's *Ghetto*, the group prepare and then assume the roles of the ghetto theatre company in Vilna, Lithuania 1943. They are ordered to prepare a revue to raise the morale of Nazi troops returning from Stalingrad. The teacher alternates between two roles: the first, a member of the Jewish Ghetto Council, encouraging the actors to participate as a means of preserving their usefulness to the Nazis, and therefore their lives; the second, a socialist worker who challenges the group to find a way of presenting the revue, as an act of resistance rather than as an act of collaboration. Differences of opinion amongst the actors based on political stance and personal/social histories have to be represented through the symbolic dimension.

◇ A Day in the Life

Description	This convention works backwards from an important event in order to fill in the gaps in the history of how the characters have arrived at the event. A chronological sequence is built up from scenes prepared by groups, involving the central character at various different times in the preceding twenty four hours. After the scenes are run together, each scene in the sequence is subsequently re-drafted to take into account the influence of other groups' scenes.
Cultural connections	A familiar form in novels, films and television.
Learning opportunities	Drawing attention to the influences, and exposing the forces, which drive a character to a moment of conflict or decision; emphasizing how inner conflicts and tensions shape the events and circumstances of the narrative.

Example 1. The group are working on an actual newspaper account of a young boy who committed suicide as a result of depression caused by long-term unemployment. The day is divided up, and groups bring back scenes which show: reading the newspaper at breakfast—the paper claims that thousands of jobs are vacant; visiting the job shop and not seeing any jobs; arguing with a girlfriend who has formed a new relationship with an older employed man; meeting a schoolfriend who asks for money for heroin; deciding not to steal food in a local supermarket.

◇ Hot-Seating

Description	A group, working as themselves, have the opportunity to question or interview roleplayer(s) who remain 'in character'. Improvisation may be frozen and roleplayer(s) released to answer questions or they may be formally seated facing questioners.
Cultural connections	Courts, inquiries; chat shows; media news; 'kiss and tell' articles; 'true life' confessions; celebrity profiles in media.
Learning opportunities	Highlighting character's motivations and personality disposition; encouraging insights into relationships between attitudes and events, and how events affect attitudes; encouraging reflective awareness of human behaviour.

Examples

1. A group have been speculating about what causes delinquency in some young adults. They have created a group of trouble-makers who are causing havoc at their school. In order to discover more about the attitudes and motivations of the trouble-makers, five volunteers take on their roles and are 'hot-seated' by the rest of the group about attitudes to school, home, family, authority, etc.

2. A group have been reading a story about a family in which the stepson asks his stepfather to persuade his mother to allow him to keep pets. The mother is very determined and takes no notice of the request; the group explore the likely conversation in pairs. Then the teacher in the role of the stepfather places himself in the middle of the circle facing an empty chair with the stepson's jacket draped on it. He is 'hot-seated' by the rest of the group role-playing the voice of the stepson probing the stepfather's failure to get through to his mother.

◇ Overheard Conversations

Description	These conversations add tension or information to a situation that should not have been heard. The group might not know who the speakers are, or might only know one of the speakers. The conversation might be reported by spies, or be in the form of gossip and rumour. The group can go backwards or forwards in time to recreate key conversations that illuminate the present situation.
Cultural connections	Spies; rumour; gossip; eavesdropping—home, street, school, café; bugging; CB radio.
Learning opportunities	Devising/interpreting conversations that are relevant; speculating on the significance of what is heard; considering the truth of rumour; adding tension and secrecy as motivation within a situation.

Examples

1. A group are speculating on the causes of civil unrest in a state that has lost confidence in its leaders. Spies are sent out into different parts of the city to eavesdrop on the citizens. They return, and report what they have heard as a way of persuading the 'Generalissimo' to take the people's problems more seriously.

2. A group, as educational psychologists, are dealing with the problem of a young black girl who is very bright but who has become totally withdrawn and aggressive. The teacher in the role of the young girl sits in the middle of the circle, while the group speaks out overheard comments/conversations about her from friends, family, teachers and social workers.

◇ Reportage

Description	This gives an interpretation/presentation of events through journalistic conventions and registers, in the manner of front-page stories, TV news or documentaries. The group may be in media roles or working outside the drama to represent what has happened from a distance, with an emphasis on how events can be distorted by outsiders.
Cultural connections	News stories; headlines; investigative journalism; tabloid press; radio bulletins; journalistic language; personal experience of the press at work.
Learning opportunities	Translation of events into news, selection of appropriate language and register; layout of headlines, story, picture; contrasting media genres—tabloid v. 'quality' press; TV v. radio.

Examples

1. A village is under threat from a proposed hydro-electric scheme. As a means of distancing them from their roles as villagers affected by the proposal, the group are re-framed as journalists who are personally unaffected by the proposal, but who have the job of presenting both sides of the argument and reporting on the CEGB's publicity campaign and the villagers' protest activity.

2. A group working on World War I have been shown a photo of a very young soldier who is apparently shell-shocked and is staring blankly into space. They presen still-images of 'what that soldier might be seeing in his mind'—images of the trenches, of death, of families waiting for news. The group are framed as journalists who have returned from the Front with these 'photographs'. The editor complains that they are 'unpatriotic' and bad for national morale. A discussion as to the role of the press in wartime follows within the drama.

◇ Noises Off

Description	The tension and motivation for the drama result from a sense of threat or danger which is imminent but not actually present. The group work with/against an imagined presence e.g. they hide from an imagined enemy, or prepare for an important visitor. They are given orders/instructions from someone outside the drama who they never meet face to face.
Cultural connections	Bogeymen; escape stories; following orders; 'outside pressure' conventions in theatre and media drama.
Learning opportunities	Problem-solving and decision-making under pressure; co-operating to overcome a threat or perform a task; a good way of heightening tension and providing motivation.

Examples

1. A group is working on the story of Ishi—the last 'wild' American Indian—who was kept as an exhibit in a museum for four and a half years from 1911. A curators, they know that Ishi is coming but they have never met him. The task is to arrange the museum for his arrival and speculate on how he should be approached/looked after. The motivation for the work comes from a character who is not actually present but whose imminent arrival creates the tension for the drama.

2. Working in role as skilled craftspeople in a hand-made furniture factory, the group receive news that the company has been taken over by a larger company specializing in mass-produced furniture and that the factory will be automated. The teacher, as intermediary, explains that there will be lay-offs but that some workers will be kept on as machine minders.

◇ Teacher-in-Role

Description	The teacher, or whoever is taking responsibility as facilitator for the group, manages the theatrical possibilities and learning opportunities provided by the dramatic context from *within* the context by adopting a suitable role in order to: excite interest, control the action, invite involvement, provoke tension, challenge superficial thinking, create choices and ambiguity, develop the narrative, create possibilities for the group to interact in role. The teacher is not acting spontaneously but is trying to mediate her teaching purpose through her involvement in the drama.
Cultural connections	Umpires/referees; team captains; coaches/trainers; other adults who involve themselves in young people's play; artists-in-residence; other forms of open-ended interactive learning.
Learning opportunities	Working with the teacher on the inside of the drama, with learning being negotiated in role; chance for students and teacher to lay aside their actual roles and take on role relationships which have a variety of status and power variables.

Example 1. The teacher initiates a drama about images of teenage disability in the following way. An empty chair is placed in a circle; the group are asked to imagine that the chair is a wheelchair seen by its owner, John, as a possible block to him being as free as others. The teacher enters the circle in the role of Julie, a friend of John. She reads an imaginary letter (cf. **Unfinished Materials**) and asks the group to assess the relationship. The letter tells John that Julie is unhappy with the relationship, feels pressured and, as a result, won't go with him to a party on Saturday.

The teacher has composed and read the letter so that it creates the possibility of ambiguity about Julie's motives. Is it because she is embarrassed about her relationship when her friends are around? Is it because she is struggling to find the courage to deepen her relationship with John? Is it because John has spoilt a friendship by expecting more emotional commitment from Julie than she is prepared to give?

The group use **Forum-Theatre** to select and explore key moments which might reveal this ambiguity:

☐ Julie and John meeting Julie's friends while out shopping; exploration of Julie's and her friends' attitudes to John;

☐ Julie and John alone in John's house; exploration of what Julie means by being pressured.

The teacher maintains the role of Julie in order to sustain the ambiguity and develop it in response to the students' handling of the situations. Various members of the group take the roles of John and others in each scene and are challenged/supported by the teacher (both in role as Julie and out of role as facilitator) as to the image of John they project.

The drama culminates in the party. The group decide on where John and Julie are placed, and then the party is improvised. The teacher uses the role of Julie as a way of encouraging the group to reconcile their understanding of the relationship through their roles as guests at the party by interacting with each other and with John and Julie.

C. Poetic Action

Montage
Role-Reversal
Forum-Theatre
Small-Group Play-Making
Re-enactment
Ritual
Analogy
Come on Down!

Masks
Caption-Making
Prepared Roles
Mimed Activity
Ceremony
Folk-Forms
Revue

Uses

These conventions are useful as a means of looking beyond the story-line, or as a means of making a deliberate shift from the realism of narrative conventions to conventions which heighten awareness of form and which allow for the exploration and representation of key symbols and images suggested by the work. The effect of moving into poetic action is often to:

☐ bring a fresh perspective to work which is becoming stale or dominated by plot-level thinking;

☐ open up an alternative channel of communication which works at the level of symbolic interpretation;

☐ increase emotional involvement.

Cultural origins

These are drawn from performing arts conventions and either make an elastic, often stylized, use of time, space and presence in order consciously to communicate symbolic intent (e.g. *Masks, Ritual*) or are used out of their predictable context and allow for incongruities and discords (e.g. *Come on Down!*)

Level of demand

Some students express a preference for working poetically—that is in an obviously theatrical way—rather than narratively, which can feel uncomfortably close to actual living. Poetic conventions often require a disciplined crafting of speech and action; the mode of communication is highly selective and bound by the constraints of the convention. Some of the conventions are complex to operate and require complex agreements about actor/spectator roles (e.g. *Montage*).

▽ Montage

Description	Montage juxtaposes form and content so as to distort or challenge a stereotypic or conventional view. It provokes a fresh look at material that may be stale and creates interesting contrasts between elements in the drama that would not naturally be brought together.
Cultural connections	Photographic montage; surrealist art; cartoons; fantasy comics; satirical drawings; posters; pop videos; film.
Learning opportunities	Reflection on and experimentation with the relationship between form and content; reconsideration of original, unquestioned interpretations of meanings through the shock of unusual or demanding combinations of form, or disparate elements of content.

Examples **1.** In a workshop looking at the social context of the 'Peterloo Massacre', different groups have been responsible for creating a 'room' in a weaver's house and one in a yeoman's house: a scene involving the weaver's family and a scene involving the yeoman's family. The work is presented in a combination of ways so that the weaver's family scene is presented in the yeoman's room and vice versa and the weaver's family scene is mimed whilst the dialogue from the yeoman family scene is heard at the same time.

2. A group are devising a documentary-drama around materials relating to World War I. They prepare a series of images that reflect the themes presented in the drama: a 'heroic' image of a war memorial is juxtaposed with a still-image of the psychological and visual reality of the war; a rugby match turns into a bayonet charge.

▽ Role-Reversal

Description	Roles are reversed as part of the action of the drama, as a play-within-a-play, and one group demonstrate to each other how they think another group or role will react e.g. bank robbers behaving as they think guards will behave; mutinous crew demonstrating how they think the captain will respond to their demands.
Cultural connections	Mimicry; imitation; conversation-in-your-head; speculating about other people's reactions; copying parents, teachers, police, etc.
Learning opportunities	Actively exploring demands and tensions presented by a future situation; way of demonstrating hypotheses about human behaviour and reactions; preparation for demanding situations; means of reflecting on problems and ways of dealing with them.

Examples **1.** In a drama concerned with the morality of Western advertising in the Third World, the group are working as a sales team for powdered baby milk. In order to fix and clarify the issues involved, the teacher-as-salesperson plays the role of a Nigerian housewife, so that the sales team can practise their sales pitch and understand some of the questions and concerns the woman might have. The teacher drops in and out of the woman's role but, when she is out of role, she is still in the role of salesperson encouraging and handling the sales team.

2. As part of their work on an 'Equal opportunities' theme, a group of male astronauts are demonstrating how they think women would handle their work. In response, a group of female astronauts demonstrate that they don't want to go into space with a man by mimicking the way they think a man would interfere with their work.

▽ Forum-Theatre

Description	A situation (chosen by the group to illuminate a topic or experience relevant to the drama) is enacted by a small group whilst the others observe. Both the actors and the observers have the right to stop the action whenever they feel it is losing direction, or if they need help, or if the drama loses authenticity. Observers may step in and take over roles or add to them.
Cultural connections	Giving/receiving advice.
Learning opportunities	Selecting appropriate situations; helping and advising each other; close attention to what is being performed; discussing and negotiating the way it would be; different attitudes to the event worked through in action.

Examples

1. A group have been looking at a family case history in which the husband has turned to drink and violent outbursts as a means of escaping his own feelings of inadequacy as father, husband and unemployed worker. The group decide to help him by sending in a YTS worker to encourage/help him to re-decorate his flat. A volunteer takes the YTS role and goes to work with the teacher-in-the-role of the husband. When he gets stuck he stops and asks for help: observers may stop him to adjust his tone and approach.

2. A group of factory workers, whose workplace is threatened with closure, go to a government office to ask for aid to keep some employment in their community. The official explains that there is limited cash available and that they will need to make out a case for being a priority. Observers help to strengthen arguments and make points.

▽ Small-Group Play-Making

Description	Small groups plan, prepare and present improvisations as a means of representing a hypothesis, or to demonstrate alternative views/courses of action. The improvisations express existing understanding of a situation or experience.
Cultural connections	Skits; sketches; TV drama; plays done at school, youth clubs, for families and friends; street theatre; theatre-in-education; assemblies.
Learning opportunities	Sequencing of ideas; selection of content; characterization; devising dialogue and events; performance skills; developing confidence in expressive performance.

Examples

1. As an introduction to work on the treatment of young offenders, the groups are asked to improvise scenes that show the various crimes that we associate with young criminals. The groups are asked to prepare carefully at least one character whose life can then be more fully explored in the subsequent drama work. The teacher expects a certain amount of stereotyping and cliché in the plays—much of the work that follows may be to do with challenging the views and ideas expressed at this stage.

2. In preparation for examining the roles and functions of the social services, groups devise scenes that demonstrate situations in which individuals or groups clearly show that they are unable to cope without some sort of support or help. Groups then discuss the social context of each situation and what sort of support service should be provided in each case.

▽ Re-enactment

Description	An event that is known, or has previously occurred, is re-enacted in order to reveal what might have happened, or in order to discover its social dynamics and tensions. There is an emphasis on accuracy of detail and authenticity. This may be a whole-group re-enactment, or small-group presentation.
Cultural connections	Reconstructions of crimes; historical dramas; closed circuit TV; film taken by spies.
Learning opportunities	Attention to detail, researching relevant data; reflecting on the event; analysing the social interactions that take place.

Examples

1. A group working on the migration of pioneers across America in the days of the wagon-trains re-enact the burial of a small baby who dies on the journey. The group bring themselves into a 'photo' taken at the moment of leaving the burial; they arrange themselves so as to represent the different attitudes towards infant mortality and the various attitudes of the people sharing the journey. Their work is based on research into the nature of the journey and the kinds of people who undertook the venture.

2. Detectives investigating a murder re-enact what they think might have happened, based on their knowledge of the victim, her background, the position she was found in and information collected since the crime.

POETIC

▽ Ritual

Description	This is stylized enactment bound by traditional rules and codes, usually repetitious and requiring individuals to submit to a group culture or ethic through their participation.
Cultural connections	Initiation into gangs; giving witness in court; elections; oath-taking in Scouts/Guides; received images of tribal societies e.g. Native Americans.
Learning opportunities	Group ideology or ethic symbolized and revealed through ritual activity ('What does this initiation tell us about the gang we're joining?'); controlled and highly structured activity requiring reflective attitude; challenging individuals within an easily followed structure.

Examples

1. A group of thirteen-year-olds are working on the theme of 'Street violence'. The context is formed from the events leading up to a clash between two rival gangs; in order to explore the differences and jealousies between the gangs, the group devise two sets of contrasting 'initiation rituals' that all gang members must undertake. Through discussion about the differences and similarities of the rituals, an understanding of the contrasting cultural and ideological stances of the two groups is established.

2. A group of space travellers have been marooned on a planet for many years. Each evening they gather to remind each other of some idea or custom from Earth that they must remember if they are to remain a civilized community. Events on the planet begin to challenge their ritual: 'To what extent are moral codes modified by environment and the need to survive?'

▽ Analogy

Description	A problem is revealed through working on a parallel situation that mirrors the real problem—usually used where the real problem is too familiar, full of prejudice or likely to make participants feel threatened or exposed; or connections are made between familiar experience and unfamiliar experience.
Cultural connections	Myths; legends; fairy stories; metaphors; similes
Learning opportunities	Creating and analysing metaphors; indirectly handling sensitive/controversial issues; making connections between analogy and real problems, encouraging reflection and providing distance for new learning about old material.

Examples

1. A drama that is actually to do with the persecution of the Jews in Nazi Germany is represented as a science fiction story concerning a group of space travellers fleeing from one planet to find another where they can be safe. A planet is selected as a new homeland, and word is sent to all who are persecuted on other planets to come to it. However, the new planet is already home to people who do not share the same beliefs as the newcomers.

2. A group of older students prepare a workshop for an infant class, focusing on green issues. They create an analogy for pollution through a legend told in polar lands. The last of the great dragons is imprisoned beneath the ice. The legend goes on to warn that: 'When the ashes fall from the south, and the snow turns to stinging rain, then the dragons will fly again.' The students have come to warn the infant 'scientists' that the prophecy is being fulfilled.

▽ Come on Down!

Description	As a way of bringing fresh insights to a passage of action that has become stale or sentimental, a radical shift of style is introduced so that the action is translated into a popular form such as a game show format, circus routine, chat show, soap opera, pop video, etc.
Cultural connections	Immediate experience of examples such as those given above.
Learning opportunities	Reveals implicit style of original action through contrast with popular style introduced; forces re-examination of values in original action as well as those embedded in popular form itself; needs a selective translation of original action into the constraints of new form.

Examples

1. In *Trafford Tanzi* Claire Luckham translates issues relating to gender and gender expectations into the form of a wrestling match.

2. A group working on the theme of 'Education' represent the pressures of the examination testing system through the form of a horse race, complete with appropriate hurdles, obstacles and commentary.

3. As part of an issue-based drama looking at housing problems faced by ethnic minority groups, events are acted out in the manner of a Chinese Monkey legend, an Anansi story and as part of the Ramayana.

▽ Masks

Description	These are sometimes seen as being useful solely for presentational work, but have rich potential for changing perspectives of situations and encounters. There is a wide variety of masks—full, half, character, anonymous, etc. which can be made economically by students themselves.
Cultural connections	Fancy dress parties; dances; the desire to create fear, horror and laughter in a safe way; the need to be ridiculous and incongruous in familiar situations; rituals and ceremonies where the personalities of the protagonists are less significant than the attitudes they portray; make-up.
Learning opportunities	Masks create a different kind of distance and alienation from the other conventions, causing the observer to 'look' differently and the participant to consider his/her contribution carefully; exploration of the incongruous and the grotesque; enhancement of perception of ritual.

Examples

1. The class adopt the roles of a fictitious 'universal' community in order to explore the hypothetical fears, dreams and hopes of such a tightly-knit group and understand the roots and causes of such emotions. The community have a ritualistic gathering together when stories from the past are told and exchanged; this ritual is carried out with the groups wearing simple masks so that the content of the stories is not diminished by a close association with the real personality of the teller. After the stories have been told, the issues within them are explored.

2. The class explore a situation where a grandmother, unable to cope, places an advertisement in a newsagent's shop, offering her daughter's illegitimate child for adoption. The scene in the shop is played out, first naturalistically, then with masks.

3. In a devised performance project, based on the growing plight of young, homeless people, the group use neutral half-masks for all authority roles as a way of symbolizing their view of the vast imbalance of power between the individual and the machinery of the state.

▽ Caption-Making

Description	Groups devise slogans, titles, chapter headings and verbal encapsulations of what is being presented visually. They are asked to crystallize their work within a phrase; or to work to a given title; or summarize a scene in words; or to fit a caption to another group's work.
Cultural connections	Advertisements; posters; jingles; episode titles on TV series; portrait and sculpture titles; song titles; album titles; chapter headings.
Learning opportunities	Precision of description; selection of appropriate form and language; making a reflective analysis of experience in order to identify its essence; summarizing experience.

Examples

1. In an investigative drama looking at recruitment into the armed services, a group devises World War I recruitment posters, after considering authentic examples. As each group shows their posters, the observers have to suggest captions for the image presented. The same exercise is repeated in relation to present-day advertisements, so that a comparison between recruitment in wartime as opposed to peacetime can be considered.

2. In a drama concerned with the strains within a family, the group create an image to represent a family photograph (i.e. the public image the family wish to project). They then devise different captions for the photo, representing the contrasting viewpoints on the public image held by various members of the family.

▽ Prepared Roles

Description	Another teacher, parent, student or older pupil is brought into the drama to play a role accurately and authentically, i.e. he/she never comes out of role. The teacher's task is to facilitate the group's meeting with this role, and to involve the group in exploring his/her life-style, problems, needs and challenges.
Cultural connections	Strangers; helping people in need; visitors to school; eccentrics in the community; meeting people from other cultures.
Learning opportunities	Using someone who strongly represents another life-style is a very powerful visual aid for work; provides own focus and tension; makes immediate emotional and intellectual demands on the group, i.e. the role will not go away and come back later; shifts emphasis onto a weighing of human relationships.

Examples

1. The teacher wants to work by appealing to young people's 'natural' wish to help those in trouble. The group are framed as medical/social workers by the teacher-in-the-role of a doctor who introduces them to a young woman (another teacher in the prepared role) sitting hunched up, distressed, nervous and clutching something in her hand. The doctor explains that the woman has been found sitting by the canal and has been brought in, but that he has been unable to communicate with her. Can they help?

2. A group of fourth-years prepare, in great detail, to represent a wandering, hungry tribe of American Indians. The 'tribe' are taken to a local special school, where they are met by a group of children who look after them and eventually join their tribe. The teacher takes the role of a land-owner who wants the tribe off his estate.

▽ Mimed Activity

Description	This activity emphasizes movement, actions and physical responses rather than dialogue or thoughts. It may include speech as an aid to enactment, encouraging a demonstration of behaviour rather than a description of it.
Cultural connections	Silent films; archive material; dance forms; dreams; charades; mime games; documentaries with voice-over commentaries; crowds in the street, market; football matches.
Learning opportunities	Busy, active convention; selecting movements to match action; removes pressure of dialogue; encourages gestures and body language; useful way of establishing a context, i.e. workers on a production line, miners working a coal face; may be stylized, accentuating movement through dance, emphasizing meanings underlying actions; impulsive/aggressive responses can be controlled by slowing mime down.

Example 1. A group working on the origins of the General Strike devise mimed activities to show aspects of a miner's life. They act as if they are archivists finding film clips to form the introduction to a TV programme on the strike. The film clips are devised at life-rate and show miners cutting the coal face, visits from the tally-man, descending in the cage, mourning families at the pit-head after a disaster. The clips are then enacted simultaneously in slow motion whilst the teacher sings 'The Gresford Disaster'.* The effect of the slow motion and the song is to draw attention to the significance of the actions and what they represent.

* *Delights and Warnings*, J. and G. Beer (Macdonald)

▽ Ceremony

Description	Groups devise special events to mark, commemorate or celebrate something of cultural/historical significance.
Cultural connections	Weddings; funerals; remembrance days; feasts; birthdays; passing-out parades; prize-givings; street spectacles.
Learning opportunities	Devising appropriate activity to mark something that has occurred or is about to occur in the drama; may involve performance work; reflective attitude combined with celebratory experience; easily controlled, structured activity; involvement of whole group simultaneously; useful as a conclusion or review of work done.

Examples

1. In a drama looking at 'The effects of change', a group 'build' a village under threat from a hydro-electric scheme. In order to give the group sense of a village's history they are asked to devise a ceremony to celebrate the unveiling of a newly commissioned war memorial. The work includes making images to represent the memorial, writing captions for it, devising speeches choosing the music/songs to be played, devising contrasting contributions from young people, veterans and newcomers to the village.

2. During a sequence of work focusing on the effects of imprisonment on women and their families, groups representing the family, friends and the community are asked to devise a 'Coming Home' celebration for a woman who was imprisoned for the manslaughter of a man who had attacked her children. In devising the ceremony, the group have to bear in mind the personality of the woman, her crime, the effects of imprisonment and expectations about her future.

▽ Folk-Forms

Description	The group may devise traditional art forms for imagined cultures e.g. how a tribe might celebrate the birth of a new queen; or an imagined folk-form may be used as a way of introducing a new drama; or the group may work within an existing folk-form in order to discover the culture it represents, or to understand the experiences described in the folk-form.
Cultural connections	Myths; legends; shanties; folk songs; Morris dancing; primitive painting; folk music; traditional dances; ethnic forms; rock and roll; jive and bop, etc.
Learning opportunities	Working within structure and limitations of traditional form; empathizing and identifying with alien historical and cultural contexts through the involvement with appropriate art forms; exploring class and culture through working-class and minority forms.

Examples

1. A group of scientists are living through an experiment to see how primitive people survived in wilderness conditions. Rather than recording their adventures and researches in diaries and tape recordings, they decide to enact them through folk-forms they imagine the tribe would have used to record and express significant events in their lives.

2. A group working on the history of mining and mining communities mime action to represent themes in songs such as 'The Gresford Disaster', 'The Collier's Rant' and 'The Collier's Wife's Lament'. The action is performed whilst the teacher sings the songs.

▽ Revue

Description	This is a sequence of scenes or performance elements, which may or may not be loosely linked, providing an overview of social conditions and human attitudes. This overview is provided without the need to relate the parts selected to a unified plot or story-line and without the need to determine a common performance style or form.
Cultural connections	Stand-up comedians; TV programmes e.g. *Monty Python, Friday Live.*
Learning opportunities	Gaining a sense of the broad sweep of events, their relationship to individuals, and the social framework which has given rise to them.

Examples

1. A group working on a project on civil liberties devise a series of short scenes and sketches exploring recent/projected Government legislation e.g. Section 28, Education Reform Act, etc.

2. As a way of sharing their understanding of the cultural diversity of their school, a group devise a celebration of these differences using representative multi-cultural extracts from rituals, stories, folk-forms, etc.

D. Reflective Action

> **Marking the Moment**   **Gestalt**
> **Moment of Truth**   **This Way/That Way**
> **Narration**   **Giving Witness**
> **Thought-Tracking**   **Voices in the Head**

Uses

These conventions are used when there is a need to stand aside from the action and to take stock of the meanings or issues that are emerging, or as a means of reviewing and commenting on the action. They provide a means for the group to articulate what characters are thinking or to give a 'psychological commentary' affording insight into the physical action. The conventions provide the same opportunity as 'soliloquy' and 'reported speech' in lyric theatre.

Cultural origins

They are drawn from theatre, film and radio conventions where the pace of the action is broken or interrupted in order to let a psychological perspective through. There tends to be a slower than natural use of time and a deliberate use of space and objects to create a reflective atmosphere.

Level of demand

Many of the conventions require personal commitment and a level of seriousness and sensitivity which can be difficult for some students to sustain. Reflective language and action depend on being able to abstract and communicate subjective responses to the drama. Some of the conventions require complex agreements e.g. where spectators may be offering the thoughts of the actors as the actors portray the physical action.

□ Marking the Moment

REFLE ■

Description	This is used as a reflective device to 'mark' a position or a moment in the drama where a feeling is aroused, or an understanding of the issue occurs. Individuals (in groups or solo) use other conventions to express that feeling or understanding or to explore further that position or moment.
Cultural connections	Poems, stories, pictures made in response to an important event—death, birthday, first kiss, being bullied, being let down, political event; commemorative photos, newspapers, memorials; civic sculptures, heroic verse, images, etc.
Learning opportunities	Choosing and expressing own moment of focus in the drama; finding form for personal feelings and thoughts; 'concretizing' reflection and analysis through expression; encouraging sensitive awareness of work.

Example 1. As the culmination of several weeks' work exploring various aspects of World War I, the group return to the position and place in the drama studio where they feel their own moment of new understanding occurred. Some 'mark' the trenches, some recruitment, some receiving letters, some learning new work skills, some a song. Groups talk about the moment they have chosen and then represent their understandings and feelings through still-images, poems, improvisations, dance/mime.

REFLE■CTIVE

☐ Moment of Truth

Description	This is a means of resolving a drama, with reflective discussion on the events used as a basis for predicting a crucial final scene. Volunteers spontaneously act out this key moment of tension involving the main protagonists, with a view to establishing for the rest of the group what would happen in reality, rather than trying to create the moment to be entertaining or theatrical. The scene is played with different volunteers until the group are satisfied that the moment is truthful.
Cultural connections	'Cinéma Vérité'; documentary; watching sporting events; observation of real life events.
Learning opportunities	Allows participants to synthesize their understanding of the drama into action rather than discussion; tests out prejudices and assumptions in action; emphasizes the effect of context on human actions; encourages a critical attitude towards the personal and social influences of class, gender, race, ability.

Examples

1. Having explored the social and economic differences between the weaver and yeoman classes at the time of the Peterloo Massacre, the group test out what would have happened if a yeoman and a weaver had crossed each other in a narrow alleyway the night before the massacre. They use chairs to mark the alleyway, and volunteers represent a weaver and a yeoman who walk towards the alleyway, arriving at the same moment. The rest of the group suggest their thoughts as they walk. The moment of truth is for the volunteers to decide and demonstrate who would have given way and why.

2. In a drama which explores a dilemma faced by a girl out shopping with her best friend, the friend steals a jersey and leaves the shop without her. The girl is stopped by a store detective and asked for her friend's name and says she will be prosecuted as an accomplice if she doesn't give the name. The group try out alternatives as to what might happen when the two friends next meet.

☐ Narration

Description	This can be in or out of the dramatic context. The teacher/leader might provide a narrative link, atmosphere or commentary, initiate a drama, move the action on, create tension; or the participants might report back in story form, providing narrative to accompany action—'we came to the river and saw that the bridge had been destroyed, so we . . .'
Cultural connections	Key moments of children's play—'I'm dead now, but when you come in I'll come alive and then we'll look for the others'; the need, on an adult level, to prepare for experiences by talking them through first e.g. meetings when one wants to focus on the real issues.
Learning opportunities	Provides information in familiar form with affective resonance; gives shape and form to activity; arouses curiosity and interest; emphasizes sense of atmosphere, place, poetic description; involves feelings and moods; activity controlled by the content and form of the narration.

Examples

1. As part of a drama where a group of scientists are living as a primitive community, the scientists enact their day's research while one member of the group re-tells the events in narrative form.

2. A group of scientists are preparing to investigate a UFO that has landed in a remote place. As they walk slowly towards the object, the teacher uses narration to slow down the pace, create the atmosphere of the moment, suggest the scientists' attitudes and expectations, build tension and belief into context.

3. In a drama about a 'disturbed child', the group enacts an event from the child's school life whilst alternative narrations are offered: the teacher's story, the child's story, the friend's story. Contrasts between viewpoints are high-lighted in the differences between the various stories and between the stories and the action we see.

☐ Thought-Tracking

Description	This reveals publicly the private thoughts/reactions of participants-in-role at specific moments in the action so as to develop a reflective attitude towards the action and to contrast thinking-for-self with outward appearances or dialogue. Action may be frozen and participants 'tapped for thoughts', or thoughts may be prepared to go with the presentation of still images.
Cultural connections	Secrets; fears; hopes; keeping up appearances.
Learning opportunities	Devising thoughts requires reflection and analysis of situation and role; hearing other thoughts generates a sensitive/feeling response to the content; action is slowed down to allow for deeper understanding of meanings underlying action.

Examples

1. A group is working on a 'Runaway' theme that emphasizes different viewpoints—those of parents, young people, public services, voluntary organizations, etc. A father comes to London to look for his daughter and discovers that she is in intensive care, suffering from hypothermia after sleeping rough. The group create an image representing what the father sees as he opens the door to her hospital room. He is accompanied by a friend of his daughter and a social worker. Also in the room are doctors, both experienced and student, nurses, a priest and a reporter who has been following her story. As the father enters, the action is frozen and each person speaks out loud his/her private thoughts/reactions.

2. As part of a sequence of work looking at 'Evacuees', half the group mime packing their bags with a parent in preparation for leaving; the other half speak out what the participants might be thinking as they pack

☐ Gestalt

Description	Following some initial work on a character, and prior to exploring that character's response to the core situation of a drama, the group split into pairs and devise dialogues which involve the protagonist and another character at a key moment in the protagonist's life. This can be taken from events real or imagined, past or future. The pair decide the most likely context and the most suitable role for the chosen moment by analysing the character's current disposition. It may well be that the core event is already known to the group—in which case future-based dialogues should take on implications of the event itself.
Cultural connections	Narrative device in literature; film conventions in which a number of actors are used to play the same character from youth to old age.
Learning opportunities	Requires extrapolation from detailed analysis of known character traits; provides opportunities for insight into the development of individual motivation, attitudes and values against the wider canvas of a variety of social interactions and perspectives; allows for appraisal of these factors and provides a more complex and rounded character for further exploration.

Example 1. In a drama dealing with the issue of 'capital punishment', the teacher chooses to build work around the 1950s Craig and Bentley murder case, which resulted in the mentally retarded Bentley being hanged. The group intend that a key moment in the drama will be the reading of Bentley's last letter to his family. To build towards this moment the group devise encounters exploring the protective attitudes of Bentley's family, his exploitation, his peer-group relationships, his gauche behaviour with members of the opposite sex and his fear of authority figures e.g. prison warder, defence counsel, etc. These improvisations are finally orchestrated by a group member in role as Bentley, animating extracts from the work of each pair by standing silently with them.

REFLE■ CTIVE

☐ This Way/That Way

Description	This is used as a means of pointing out the differences between various characters' interpretations of the same crucial event and thereby demonstrating that the points of view held may reflect the vested interests of the characters. The group act out each character's version of the event, paying attention to the detail of the differences and relating these details back to their understanding of the character.
Cultural connections	Witnesses for defence/prosecution in court-cases; differences in newspaper accounts; party-political broadcasts; tall stories; 'who otartod it in thc firot placc?', ctc.
Learning opportunities	Allows group to detect and deconstruct the level of bias and prejudice in accounts given of the same event; encourages examination of the effect of class, race and gender interests on individual perspectives.

Examples **1.** The group are using the following statement by Yellow Wolf of the Nez Percés as a starting point for looking at the colonization of the American West: 'The whites told only one side. Told it to please themselves. Told much that is not true. Only his own best deeds, only the worst deeds of the Indians, has the white man told.'

2. As part of an investigative drama inquiring into the causes of a violent incident at a local colliery, the group act out the event according to the conflicting accounts given in the press and in person by the national and local newspapers, the colliery manager, a picket and the local police.

☐ Giving Witness

Description	Teacher-in-role, or other individual, gives a monologue purporting to be an objective account of events, but which in effect is a highly subjective re-telling from the witness' point of view. The account is often charged with emotion—in the manner of oral history, evidence in court or inquiry.
Cultural connections	Oral histories—family, read in books; courtroom dramas in media; hearing different accounts of the same event e.g. own, teacher's, friend's; TV chat shows; monologues in media drama; working-class history; memoirs.
Learning opportunities	Combining information with affective response; identifying and establishing bias and prejudice; linking events to cultural and class environment; linking attitudes to events; shaping stories to match the teller.

Examples **1.** In a study of 'The Crucible', the group first hear a re-telling of a witch hunt by the mother of the victim, and then by the father. Other individuals, more or less affected by the events, give their re-telling as if it was some time later when they have had the chance to reflect. These monologues are then set against the way the same witnesses gave evidence at the 'witch's' trial. The group arrive at an idea of the people involved from a discussion of the subjectivity contained in each account and what it tells us about the witness.

2. A group is looking at the effects of persecution and prejudice on a group of people who have been forced to flee their planet to find freedom. Several generations later they participate in a 'remembrance moot' at which the youngest member of each family re-tells an oral history of the persecution as it has been passed down through the family 'lest they forget'.

REFLECTIVE

☐ Voices in the Head

Description	The group use this as a means of reflecting on the complexity of a difficult choice facing a character in the drama—others represent and speak as the possibly conflicting thoughts of the character at that moment, or act as a collective conscience which gives the character advice based on moral or political choices.
Cultural connections	Own experience of 'voices in the head'; voice-over in film, television e.g. *Rockford Files, Magnum*; use of 'asides' in theatre.
Learning opportunities	Character becoming more aware of the problem faced, others express, become involved in and influence the complexity of the imminent action; adds tension and slows action down to allow for greater reflection.

Examples

1. In a drama concerned with a young Afro-Caribbean girl's struggle to overcome the physical threat of a gang of white boys, the girl has to choose to walk home the long way round or take the shortest route which will mean facing the gang. The rest of the group arrange themselves so that they physically represent the 'cross-road' where the choice needs to be made. The girl is placed in the centre of the 'cross-road'. The others give guidance to the girl according to their place on the 'long route' or the 'short route'.

2. The boyfriend of a girl, who is struggling with choices about her sexuality, determines to force himself physically on her. The group form themselves into a narrow twisting corridor leading to the girl's room. The girl is placed at the end of the corridor. The boyfriend makes his approach down the corridor and the group represent the conflict in his conscience as he passes through.

3. A group are exploring the pressures which might cause a young person to leave her home town. The girl finds herself sitting at the station, unsure of whether to go or stay. The rest of the group speak to her as the voice of her mother, her friend, her teacher/employer and others who might influence her choice.

4. As a way of exploring the gap between what is said and what is meant in an argument between a girl and her mother, two 'shadows' stand with the characters and speak out the girl's and the mother's thoughts during the dialogue.

Part 2 Structuring Drama for Learning Opportunities

■ Introduction

The conventions outlined in the previous section give some indication of the forms available for working through theatre. The purpose of this section is to identify possible **processes** which may enable students and teachers/leaders to make creative use of the conventions in order to create opportunities for learning. The processes described in this section are based on a set of common assumptions about theatre as a learning medium, the purposes of a 'conventions approach' to learning through theatre, and principles of practice which guide structuring drama for learning opportunities.

■ Assumptions about Theatre Processes and Forms

■ Historically, theatre has always drawn its content from a broad sweep of human experience. Its conventions have evolved through the need to provide entertainment and illumination through the accurate, critical, and sensuous depiction of individuals and groups engaged in the business of living in the world, within a variety of socio-historical contexts.

■ In common with other narrative forms, like story and film, theatre frames and represents aspects of human experience and social concepts through the isolation and portrayal of specific examples which are representative of a broader area of human experience. The success of a theatrical activity is partly judged on its ability to subsume an important area of human experience within a particular set of fictional circumstances, situations and characters.

■ Theatre triggers similar psychological processes to other narrative art forms, such as novels, poetry and film. In other words, it harnesses the basic, natural and spontaneous human ability to make and respond to stories, told in words and pictures, which help a storyteller to symbolize her sense of the world and an audience to see and hear the world from another's perspective.

■ In order to make its stories, or 'representations of experience', the conventions of theatre utilize dimensions of form which are shared with conventions in other art-forms as well as dimensions which are unique to theatre:

1. Language

☐ In common with most other art-forms, language is used in theatre as the organizing medium for discussing, planning and implementing ideas; group work comes out of talk about the task, a director will use language to describe ideas to actors. Language is also used symbolically as a means of representing a situation or a character's speech (as it might also be used in the narrative forms of story, prose, poetry and film).

☐ However, theatre does not wholly depend on the symbolic use of language in the same way narrative forms (other than film) do in order to describe places, relationships, or action. A **Still-Image** for example, uses space, gesture and objects, rather than words, to represent places, relationships and action. Because theatre is a visual as well as an aural medium, meanings are often communicated through an inter-play between what is seen and what is said.

2. Relationships of time

☐ In common with other narrative forms, the way in which certain conventions interact with the experience of time is a central feature of theatre-form. In literary forms, narrative sometimes follows a natural sequence of time where one event follows another chronologically, but it can also use conventions that fracture and distort a natural sequence—flash backs/forwards; letters; third-person commentary, etc. In theatre the same is true: time either unfolds at life-rate or is taken to be a completely elastic material that can be stopped, accelerated and replayed through the use of conventions.

☐ The experience of time in theatre is distinguished by the fact that 'action' in other narrative forms (novels, poems, film) is usually reported and past for the reader whereas action in theatre is always in the 'here and now' for the audience and actors (even if the action belongs to an historical event). Because theatre is a narrative form, the here-and-now experience of a dramatic moment is enhanced by the expectation that something else is about to happen; interest in the here-and-now is held by the promise of what begins to happen next. Theatre is live, but it is also transient and ephemeral; it only exists for as long as the performance lasts. It is not permanent in the way that film and other recorded narrative forms are.

3. Relationships of space

☐ Certain conventions focus on the symbolic use of space in order to convey meanings either in terms of movements in space, as in dance, or in the way in which space is arranged and used to provide a visual context, or reinforcement, for meanings associated with levels of status between characters, physical surroundings, and psychological distance in relationships.

☐ The relevance of space to meaning-making in theatre is evidenced in scripts where 'directions' are given to indicate to actors appropriate moves and gestures to accompany dialogue. The importance of space is also evidenced in the term 'Scene' which associates a section of action with a place or use of space. In performance there is often a division of space which defines an acting area; the expectation is that any movement or use of space in the defined area will be symbolic and meaningful for the spectators.

☐ In improvisation work space may be used more intuitively, with an emphasis on discovering the possibilities of space as the drama unfolds, but awareness of how space is being used is still profoundly important to the meaning-making process and to helping participants build confidence in the drama. The question of how the available space might be used to give additional meaning to the action, or to build the participants' belief in the action, is as important as questions to do with role and situation.

4. Social interaction

☐ As in certain kinds of music activity and in dance, theatre is a social and collective form which depends on the creative interaction between the skills of actors/spectators/writers/technicians/designers/directors. Interaction occurs in two dimensions:

a) The *real dimension* of discussion, planning, organizing and reviewing;

b) The *symbolic dimension* when participants are interacting and behaving symbolically within a convention which temporarily supersedes the real dimension.

Immediately before going on stage actors may interact in the real dimension, but once on stage they can only communicate through the words and actions of their characters. Actors faced with a problem in the real dimension whilst on stage (such as might be caused by the non-appearance of a vital prop or another character skipping a scene) will struggle to manage the real problem by improvising with each other in character within the symbolic dimension.

This experience of managing the real dimension from within the symbolic dimension is central to the learning experience of improvisational forms of drama. The challenge and thrill for groups in conventions such as **Teacher-in-Role, Meetings, Hot-Seating** and **Voices in the Head** is that they have to manage signals and communications in the real dimension from within the convention. Real anxieties or questions have to find expression through the symbolic dimension if the convention is to be sustained. For example, an individual may be confused by the identity of a character who is being Hot-seated. Rather than breaking the convention, a question has to be asked, in context, to reveal the character's identity without forcing the character to break and respond in the real dimension. This subtle interchange between the real and symbolic, which is necessary to the successful management of improvisational conventions, makes substantial demands on groups but also provides substantial rewards.

In the symbolic dimension channels of communication and the participants' behaviour are deliberately limited by the nature of the conventions which are being used to create meaning. In **Small-Group Play-making**, for instance, the actors are confined to speech and behaviour which belongs to the characters and action they are representing, and the spectators are confined to wait until the actors have finished before commenting. In **Forum-Theatre**, on the other hand, the convention allows the spectators to interrupt and comment on the action as it unfolds, and the actors agree to be influenced by the spectators' suggestions and modelling.

■ Assumptions about Purpose

■ The learning potential of theatre, as an arts-process, lies in the students' conscious and critical realization of the relationships created between the content-area of a drama (some aspect of human experience) and the conventions used to engage with that content. Therefore, knowledge of the conventions is useful only in so far as it enables meaningful content to be productively 'handled', demonstrated and experienced by those taking part in the dramatic activity. Within this view, the conventions of theatre are seen as vehicles for experiencing and communicating meanings symbolically. Using the matching of convention to content in order to depict and transform personal and social meanings is the process of theatre.

■ Knowledge and understanding of the ways in which conventions and content interact in theatre allow students to develop a critical consciousness of the work of playwrights and the ideological bias within different styles and genres of theatre.

■ An imaginative and tuned awareness of the possibilities of the conventions, and the demands made by them allows students to isolate and simulate aspects of human experience for themselves. Increasingly abstract and complex concepts can be made concrete, communicable and open to examination through the student's discovery and experience of different matches of convention and content. *The effect of the experience of translating ideas and concepts into 'here-and-now' symbolic action is to transform pre-existing thinking about the content.*

■ Principles for Structuring Theatre for Learning Opportunities

The brief set of principles below are used to guide the presentation of the approach to structuring suggested in this section as they might also be able to guide choices in the development of an improvised drama activity. They are based on the assumption that structures must alter and change according to circumstances rather than remain as rigid templates which ignore the here-and-now potential of theatre experience. Even in the performance of a 'fixed' text, the structure will be influenced by the experience of the actors, the responses of the audience, the venue and unforeseen circumstances. In improvised forms of drama, choices about how the drama might develop are a constant feature and it is useful to have a consistent set of principles to assist in making the appropriate choice of direction or action.

■ Structuring should observe the agreed rights and dignity of those taking part and those who are represented in the work in both real and symbolic dimensions; at the very least this means matching conventions and content so as to remove, disturb and inhibit prejudicial and disempowering images of class, race and gender.

■ Choices about which conventions are used and which content is explored should respect the teacher's/leader's need to ensure that the work is controlled, purposeful and effective. (Different conventions pose different kinds of risk and demand for both students and the teacher/leader.)

■ Systematic opportunities should be provided for students to make informed choices about conventions, content, structure and the meanings suggested by the work.

■ Structuring should take into account the need to introduce conventions within the context of content relevant to, and representative of, the group's needs and current preoccupations.

■ Structuring should combine personal and social learning arising from the content with aesthetic learning about the conventions of theatre.

■ Students should see theatre as a powerful vehicle for challenging and changing attitudes towards the world and for the expression of a world view.

■ The dramatic activity should be punctuated by systematic and structured opportunities for personal, small-group and whole-group reflection that focuses on the personal and social demands made by the work in terms of:

☐ exploring the moral, political, social and historical meanings emerging from the dramatic exploration of the content-area;

☐ understanding the changing effect the use of different conventions is having on the content (or on the group's original responses to the content);

☐ analysing the inter-relationships between convention and content;

☐ checking out any assumptions or values held by the group, or individuals working within the group, which are biasing or prejudicing the development of the work;

☐ checking out and balancing, if necessary, the emotional and skill demands made by the convention in use.

Figure   1   A Process-model for Theatre in Educational Contexts

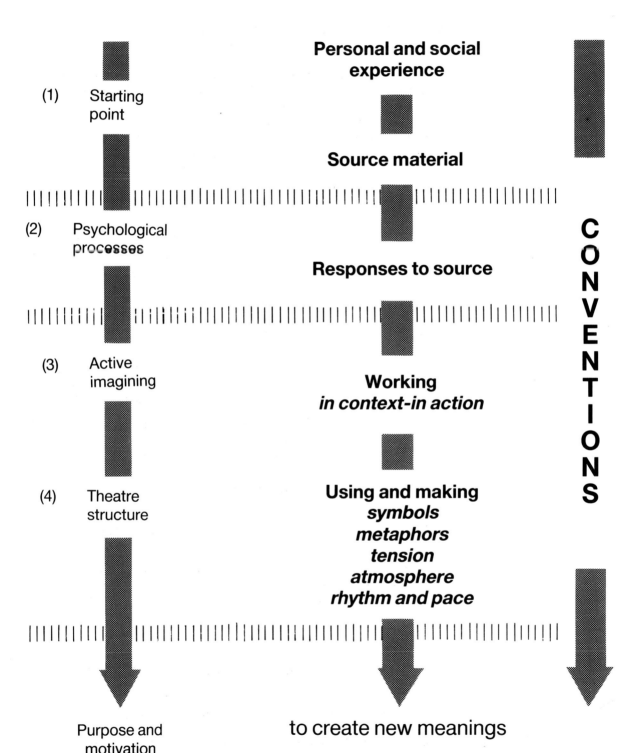

Personal and social experience

(1)   Starting point

Source material

(2)   Psychological processes

Responses to source

(3)   Active imagining

Working in context-in action

(4)   Theatre structure

Using and making symbols metaphors tension atmosphere rhythm and pace

Purpose and motivation

to create new meanings

C O N V E N T I O N S

A Process-model for Theatre in Educational Contexts (Fig. 1)

1. Starting point—identifying the content

The source material for dramatic activity of any kind will be rooted in human experience. To the individuals involved in the activity, the experience itself may be real, imagined, reported, or historical. The source material may be:

a concept, such as 'freedom';
a newspaper account;
a playscript;
facsimile documents;
an image or sculpture;
a map or diagram;
lyrics;

a story;
a photograph or painting;
a primary or secondary
   historical source;
a poem;
an object associated with
   the experience;
music and sounds;
an expression of feeling
   within the group.

The source is selected according to its ability to bring the experience into the intellectual and emotional comprehension of the participants (help the group to make human contact with the experience) so that responses and questions can be shared and some element of the experience can be located within their own personal and collective experience. Some experiences, or human concepts, may be so far removed, or so abstract, that a source is required which makes the experience manageable for participants. The biblical story of Solomon may serve as a source for an exploration of concepts of justice and fairness; *Measure for Measure* may serve as a source for exploring the power of the State and the responsibilities of leadership. (In a sense, the examples given for the conventions described in Part One serve as 'sources' for making the experience of the convention understandable and manageable for readers.)

For the dramatic activity to be worthwhile the source needs to find a response in those taking part; the experience of street theatre demonstrates that if an idea fails to interest and catch hold nobody takes part or watches. The selection and introduction of a particular source as an appropriate starting point for dramatic activity is clearly a crucial matter; in educational contexts the selection of source may be influenced by its potential to:

☐ translate a human experience accurately into terms which can be recognized and understood by the students;

☐ represent the experience in an accessible combination of words, images and feelings;

☐ immediately capture the interest and imagination of a group;

☐ give sufficient information about an experience and engage feelings;

□ speak directly to the group's current preoccupations;

□ motivate a desire to seek further information;

□ trigger the natural need to make sense of clues given in the source through the construction of stories which flesh out the clues;

□ create an appropriate background of concerns and feelings amongst the group.

2. Psychological processes—establishing ownership

Part of the process of making a response to the source involves making imaginative and quizzical connections to the words, images and feelings which the source uses in order to represent the experience to which it relates. Participants may relate to all three or they may find that individually it is easier to relate to representations in words, or in pictures, or in feelings. Because theatre is a collective and social activity, groups can pool the individual responses and work from an enhanced group response to the source. Because theatre uses words, images and feelings in its conventions it is possible, in dramatic activity, to structure opportunities for responding by using conventions which release all three in a variety of combinations; this holds for devising, interpreting script and improvised drama.

In structuring for improvised drama the teacher/leader has the advantage of being able to introduce conventions as the activity develops to match or challenge the form of a particular group's response at different points in the drama. If the group's response is in images then the teacher/leader can choose to work in visual conventions, such as **Still-image**, **Mimed Activity**. Alternatively the teacher/leader may wish to extend the response by introducing conventions which emphasize verbal communications, such as **Role-play**, **Teacher-in-Role**, **Telephone Conversations**.

3. Active imagining—from response to action

The nature of the conventions of theatre allows the participants to start using them fairly immediately in order to begin to bring the chosen experience, and their responses to it, into their own immediate 'here-and-now' experience. Agreement about an area of enquiry, a response or a particular place and moment suggested by the source (together with an agreement about the form and roles required by the convention which is to be used) allows participants to move into the symbolic dimension of theatre as a means of further developing their understanding both of the experience and of the convention. *It is an essential feature of theatre, as an educational medium, that it provides a means of bringing an experience into action and into context; it bypasses discussion and gives the signal for the participant's talk and activity to change to talk and activity which they imagine is representative of the experience itself.*

Certain conventions allow for a more immediate entry into theatre than others. For instance; the source might suggest, to the participants, possible responses to four basic questions:

☐ What questions do we want to ask?

☐ Whom do we want to question?

☐ Who might have an interest in asking the questions?

☐ Where and when would the questions be put?

These responses might lead in turn to the immediate use of:

Teacher-In-Role ◇		**Meetings** ◇	
Mantle of the Expert ◇		**Giving Witness** ☐	
Interviews/Interrogations ◇		**Forum-Theatre** ▽	
Hot-Seating ◇		**Voices in the Head** ☐	

Alternatively, the source may suggest conventions which require group talk and activity geared towards a group presentation which fixes responses to the experience through:

Still-Image ○		**Role-on-the-Wall** ○	
Simulations ○		**Re-enactment** ▽	
Diaries, Letters, Journals, Messages ○		**Costuming** ○	
A Day in the Life ◇		**This Way/That Way** ☐	
Small-Group Play-Making ▽			

Even where the entry into theatre is dependent on preliminary talk and activity, the group is immediately helped to make sense of the experience represented by the source through the preparatory work for the convention, which is context-building action, task-focused and intended to guide the group towards making the experience concrete, particular and manageable.

4. Theatre structure—generating meanings

Conventions define the form of the dramatic activity and how participants behave at particular stages of its development. *Structure describes the dynamic relationship which emerges between the stages of the drama; the relationship between conventions as the drama progresses.* The structural elements described here do not necessarily reside in separate conventions; rather they grow out of the progressive matching of conventions and content which in turn leads to a development of understanding and experience.

Symbols It is in the nature of theatre that it is understood that objects, action and use of space have the capacity to become a focus for meanings which go beyond the literal. A chair may be understood to represent a throne—which in turn may develop into a focus for the representation of the relationship between the ruler and the ruled. The chair may be re-used in a variety of conventions so that it accumulates importance as a symbol for the focus of the work. The importance of symbols lies in their capacity to go on generating further and deeper meanings as the drama develops and also in their capacity to serve as *reference points* or *motifs* which bind the various stages of the development of the drama.

Whilst all conventions (particularly poetic action conventions) have the potential to generate symbols, certain conventions tend to emphasize or produce symbols:

Ritual ▽	**Ceremony** ▽
Still-Image ○	**Defining Space** ○
Masks ▽	**Diaries, Letters, Journals, Messages** ○
Mimed Activity ▽	**Re-enactment** ▽

Atmosphere In common with other art-forms the atmosphere associated with a piece of dramatic activity is an important factor in generating responses. The construction of an appropriate atmosphere builds credibility and arouses feelings and moods which are both appropriate to the context and also experienced in a real way by both participants/actors and spectators/audience. Because theatre is always live, atmosphere has a special importance for the audience in creating levels of mood, context and circumstance.

In performance, atmosphere is generated for an audience through the tone and register of the actor's voice, the action, set and costume design, lighting, music and other effects. In improvised forms the same sources can be used to generate an appropriate atmosphere for the participants.

Certain conventions tend to emphasize and produce atmosphere:

Soundtracking ○	**Masks** ▽
Thought-Tracking in Still-Image □	**Prepared Roles** ▽
Re-enactment ▽	**Teacher-in-Role** ◇
Giving Witness □	**Hot-Seating** ◇
Ritual ▽	**Marking the Moment** □
Narration □	

Tension Tension in theatre describes the different sources of mental or emotional arousal participants or an audience might experience during dramatic activity.

As in other narrative forms, narrative-action tensions may be invitations, or lures, to become committed and involved in the unfolding story or action. For example, the tension of:

□ what will happen next;

□ a mystery;

□ a race against time;

☐ becoming dependent on a person or natural resource;

☐ a secret known to some but not to others;

☐ an obstacle to be overcome in order for a situation to be resolved;

☐ enduring a test or challenge;

☐ a moral dilemma.

Tension in poetic-action conventions may also emerge in ways that are familiar in art-forms such as music, dance and the visual arts through:

☐ counter-pointing the use of space, sounds, movements;

☐ contrasting:
   stillness/movement
   light/darkness
   sound/silence;

☐ symbols which have ambiguous or contradictory meanings.

Social Metaphor Symbolic action in theatre is understood to be representative of actions associated with actual experience. The purpose of metaphor in theatre, as in other art-forms, is to invite comparison between what is being symbolically represented and the real area of experience that is referred to. Part of the learning experience of theatre is in recognizing and constructing connections between the fiction of the drama and the real events and experiences the fiction draws on. *As the theatrical activity unfolds, the fictional situation and characters become more and more recognizable to the creators of the drama, and relationships begin to form between what is happening in the drama and what happens in the outside world.*

Rhythm and Pace As in all other art-forms the conventions of theatre give participants the opportunity to suspend reality through representative uses of time, space and behaviour. Theatre provides the opportunity to re-arrange the otherwise unalterable rhythm and pace of reality. Theatre concepts like 'timing' and 'pacing' are as important to the experience of the drama as 'pulse' and 'rhythm' are in music. Audiences talk about performances being 'slow' and actors' 'good timing'. There are other important considerations when structuring drama for learning opportunities. For example, the need to establish a rhythm and pace that:

☐ allows for reflection;

☐ moves at the right pace for all the participants to feel comfortable;

☐ provides a variety of activity, group size and conventions;

☐ balances active/still involvement and actor/spectator roles;

☐ accommodates institutional constraints on time, space, and noise levels.

Part 3 Theatre as a Learning Process

Within the presentation of theatre-process in Figure 1 (p. 62) there is an implicit suggestion of a mirror educational process which is based on the assumption that it should be geared to students experimenting with theatre in an *active inquiry mode* in order to discover more about human experience and the aesthetic possibilities of theatre through:

- ☐ the active study and performance of theatre texts;

- ☐ experiencing, as spectators and as actors, a variety of world theatre styles and genres as well as experiencing the diversity of conventions within each style;

- ☐ using conventions to experience and to translate, depict and transform personal and social meanings.

An active inquiry using theatre involves students engaging with complex areas of human experience in order to discover the questions and issues which are relevant to their needs and level of experience. The process of inquiry is cyclical and on-going because the nature of theatre is to discover and re-discover new depths in the material in focus. An actor may have played Ophelia several times, but work on a new production offers the actor the opportunity to discover new facets and ambiguities in the role. A group of students may often have worked in drama on the theme of families, but a different starting point, or a fresh match of convention to theme, offers the possibility of new areas of inquiry and understanding. Because theatre is essentially concerned with the sweep of human experience it tends to prompt new levels of questioning rather than to promote answers.

■ Theatre in an Active-inquiry Process (Fig. 2)

Figure 2 (p. 69) seeks to identify this educational process as a cyclical model based on certain key stages in the development of an active inquiry through theatre.

1. Experience/source → issue

(See also *1. Starting point—identifying the content*, p. 63)

Discussion and responses to the source will move towards the identification of those content-focused issues which will form the basis for the inquiry through theatre. The issues may relate to:

(a) *Problems of meaning—how to find depth in the source*

- ☐ questions about the logic and sequence of events described in the source;

- ☐ speculations about the wider context of the source;

Figure 2

Theatre in an Active – inquiry Process

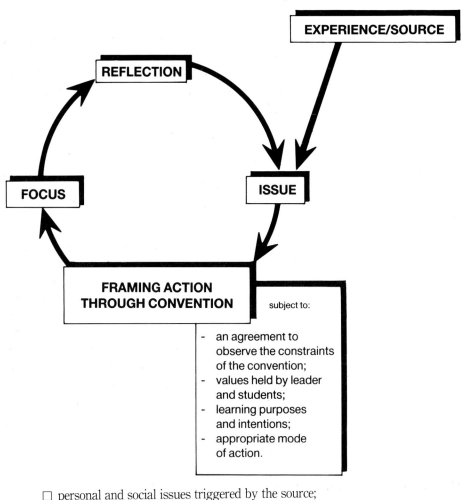

☐ personal and social issues triggered by the source;

☐ questions about motivation, intentions, consequences of actions referred to in the source;

☐ curiosities about the people and events described in the source.

(b) *Problems of form—how to translate the experience into theatre*

☐ how to stage or how to re-enact events described in the source;

☐ how to set up a situation for improvisation which will relate to the experience described in the source;

☐ how to apply techniques, skills and conventions in order to open up the material;

☐ how to find and exploit the dramatic potential in the material in order to realize and convey symbols, atmosphere, metaphor and tension.

2. Framing action through convention

(see also *3. Active imagining—from response to action*, p. 64)

This stage in the process is reached when there is sufficient commitment to the idea of exploring further the area of experience identified through the source and the group's initial responses to the source.

The transition from discussion about the issues involved to behaving and talking 'in context, in action' is a delicate shift into theatre. The success of this transition is likely to be determined by an agreement amongst the majority, if not all, of those present, to *observe the constraints* of the conventions on role behaviour and the imagined uses of time, space and presence.

Making an effective match depends on a careful consideration of a variety of factors relating to the personal, social and aesthetic needs of the group and the teacher/leader, as well as to the issue arising from the content. The choice of convention will seek an appropriate match with the issues identified, but the choice will be limited by;

☐ the values the teacher/leader seeks to promote or exclude from the inquiry;

☐ the value the students place on the process of theatre as a form of inquiry and their willingness to participate as actors and/or spectators;

☐ the learning intentions underlying the inquiry;

☐ the mode of action which is appropriate to the personal/social needs in the group and the aesthetic development of the inquiry.

Observing the Constraints—agreeing to suspend disbelief For dramatic activity of any kind to take place, participants need to agree to behave in ways which make it possible for theatre to happen. The dominant performance tradition in Western lyric theatre, for example, requires an audience who agree to remain silent, fixed and virtually invisible for the duration of the performance, and in return actors agree to confine their behaviour and talk to that which is consistent with the imagined experience they are representing for the audience. The audience agree to discuss and comment after the actors have signalled the end of their work. Each of the conventions described in this book requires participants to agree to constrain their behaviour in specific ways, and to adopt roles which reflect the roles of spectator and actor.

The nature of the agreement required will vary from one convention to another; some conventions will require subtle and complex agreements:

☐ In **Hot-Seating**, for instance, an agreement is made that one or more of the group will speak and behave as if they were roles and characters involved in the drama. The rest of the group agree either to behave as spectators by allowing the characters to speak or to ask the characters appropriate questions without challenging the illusion. The agreement may also include the idea that other participants can only ask questions which are appropriate to a particular role or viewpoint, such as scientists, detectives, newspaper reporters, etc.;

☐ In **Whole-Group Role-Play** participants agree to fuse the roles of actor and spectator so that a participant restricts herself to talk and behaviour appropriate to someone who is part of the fictional experience—even if, psychologically, she is more of a detached spectator watching and following the fictional behaviour of others who are more involved as actors. An agreement is often made to hold questions and comments belonging to the real dimension until the symbolic dimension offered by the role-play is suspended for discussion and reflection.

The agreement required by a theatre convention is more easily secured if those taking on the roles of spectators and actors have elected to be present through choice and have an inquisitive interest both in the content and in the form of the performance or dramatic experience. In educational contexts, however, this is often not the case. Within any group there may be a range—from those committed to the drama, through those who are uncomfortable with the idea, to those who are only there because they are forced to be so. The decision to proceed into dramatic action in certain educational contexts is, therefore, a difficult one to make. The decision might be influenced by evidence that:

☐ the source has aroused sufficient enthusiasm to consider suggesting theatre as a way forward;

☐ a workable proportion of the group feel ready to observe the convention that is suggested as an introduction to the dramatic work;

☐ moving into theatre is likely to increase rather than diminish a possibly low level of initial commitment to the project;

☐ an appropriate match of content and convention can be made;

☐ preliminary discussion has allowed participants to make choices between conventions suggested as starting points for the action and also to make choices about whether they wish to participate as spectators or actors;

☐ participants are clear about the intentions of the work in terms of how it might develop understanding of both convention and chosen content.

Teacher/leader values on content

An active-inquiry mode of working suggests an openness to the idea that students should discover and make their own meanings out of the content as a result of their work in drama. In practice, the range of available meanings is likely to be constrained by teacher/leader concern to filter choices about the match of convention to content in order to promote certain values through the work and also to resist the emergence of other values. There is, of course, a tradition in theatre of the voices of the playwright and director dominating the work of actors and others involved in the performance and, as a result, also dominating the range of meanings communicated to the audience. The same is inevitably true for the teacher/leader involved in the process of matching convention to content.

Improvised drama tends to allow participants a greater freedom to be actively involved in the matching process, but even so the teacher/leader may wish to avoid a match of convention to content which might produce responses which will ultimately deny the dignity of, or exclude, individuals in the group or the people they represent in the drama on the basis of gender, social class, ability, sexuality, ethnicity or age. In preventing the portrayal of deficit images the teacher/leader is also positively promoting values such as tolerance, fairness, justice, compassion, respect for others. The force of teacher/leader involvement (or lack of it) will be influenced by his/her own moral and political ideologies.

The choice of convention may also be limited in instances where the teacher/leader gauges that the material is becoming uncomfortable and over-threatening for individuals in the group, and that the use of certain conventions may increase the problem.

In very general terms, **narrative-action** *conventions, because they emphasize events and work at a relatively fast pace, may encourage superficial or poorly considered responses, whereas well-researched* **context-building action** *and the controlled pace of* **reflective action** *may produce challenges to assumptions and prejudices.*

The process of matching convention to content to the needs of the group is underpinned by the assumption that the teacher/leader is working with a consistent and explicit set of **principles** (see p. 60) which check and guide teacher/leader intervention in the students' choice of convention, and also that the teacher/leader is planning to ensure that an improvisation allows for fresh insights to be developed within a framework of constraints.

Teacher-in-role is a particularly sensitive way for the teacher/leader to initiate changes in the direction of the drama, challenges to thinking, shifts in action and new conventions from within the symbolic dimension, i.e. to manage the real needs and concerns of the group from within the drama. In an active-inquiry mode of working it is particularly important to make reference to reflective/evaluative questions which clearly indicate the level of advantage the teacher/leader is taking in the drama through **Teacher-in-Role**, and to ensure that responses to the questions are consistent with the principles.

The following questions are designed to assist teachers and students who wish to use a **Teacher-in-Role** convention as a central resource for initiating, developing and managing a drama.

■ **What information is being given?**

—about the context;

—about the situation;

—about the roles the group are being invited to adopt.

■ **What atmosphere is the role generating?**

—through selection of: vocabulary; register (linguistic); tone; category of action; volume; costume/props; spatial relationships.

■ **What doors are being opened to the group?**

—clues as to what needs doing by whom;

—a definition of the problem;

—possibilities for interaction;

—what human themes and issues are being introduced;

—indications as to what sort of 'destinations' the group might travel to in the drama.

■ **What doors are kept closed?**

—parameters of the action defined by role;

—decisions made by the teacher/leader rather than by the group in response to the role;

—clues as to who will hold the balance of power in the interaction.

■ **Where is the challenge?**

—Is a task being set?

—Is the role going to cause a disturbance within an existing situation?

—Is a request for help being made?

—What demands are going to be made on the group?

■ **What tension is being created by the role's presence?**

—What affective tension will hold the 'game' of the drama together and provide a motive for joining in? Possible tensions might include:

tension of secrecy;

tension of mystery;

tension of an obstacle to overcome;

tension of time;

tension of dare/personal challenge/test;

tension of dependence on another;

tension of status to be challenged.

■ **What controls are within the role's behaviour?**

—Are implicit/explicit 'rules' introduced by the role?

—How is the group's attention held?

—What attempts are made to focus the group's activity or verbal responses?

—Where is the source of the role's authority?

in its status;

in its situation;

in its spectacle.

Group Values on Theatre as a Learning Process

The match of convention to content also depends on the value the group places on dramatic activity as a useful and meaningful means of handling the source material. Because theatre uses the whole person for expression, there is a considerable risk for participants who cannot, without feeling threatened, let go of their concerns and pressures in the *real* dimension in order to move into the exposure of the *symbolic* dimension. Equally, individuals may be conditioned to expect theatre to be a low-level learning activity to which they find it difficult to give commitment. *Matching requires negotiation over the level of risk and commitment for which a group is prepared.*

The conventions allow for considerable flexibility over levels and degrees of involvement. Certain conventions often assume whole-group participation by limiting responses to the symbolic dimension of the drama (by only allowing responses-in-role):

Teacher-in-Role ◇   **Meetings** ◇
Still-Image ○   **Mantle of the Expert** ◇

Other conventions allow for a small group of 'actors-by-choice' and a larger group of 'spectators-by-choice' to be involved in the direction and improvisation of the drama; they also allow for the roles of spectator and actor to be picked up, exchanged and dropped when participants choose to do so:

Forum-Theatre ▽   **Hot-Seating** ◇
A Day in the Life ◇   **Voices in the Head** □
Narration □   **Moment of Truth** □
Giving Witness □

Within each convention there are further variables. For example, **Hot-seating** often suggests the idea of there being one or more actors sitting in a chair, responding to questions from a group of spectators who may or may not be in roles themselves. There may be a reason why a group does not produce any volunteers for hot-seating. If so, there are a number of variables which may assist the group's use of the convention:

□ The teacher/leader can take the role and be questioned by the group as themselves;

□ an empty chair can symbolize the role and the group can collectively respond, in the role's words, to questions asked;

□ the teacher/leader can put the questions to the empty chair and then ask the group to respond what they think the role's thinking might be, or what their own response might be.

Example 1—
Guiding values

A youth theatre group are beginning to devise a programme on issues relating to 'World Hunger'. The teacher/leader is responsible for an initial session which will put the group in touch with the issues. The teacher/leader rejects the idea of the group attempting to 'experience' hunger and the situation of refugees directly, as the group have suggested.

Instead, she uses the group's collective experience of aid-workers talking about their experiences in the media as a means of shifting the dramatic viewpoint to that of aid-workers. Three chairs are placed in an empty space which represents the inside of a tent in a camp in Somalia. Groups prepare short scenes which focus on a personal or professional event which might lead a character to decide to go to the camp as a volunteer. As each scene finishes the central character goes and sits in a chair until all the chairs are occupied.

The rest of the group form a circle around the chairs and the teacher/leader uses **Narration** to set the scene in the tent with the three newly arrived aid-workers who have flown in by night and woken to wait for the camp co-ordinator. The rest of the group are asked to try to supply a **Soundtracking** of the noises and sounds of the camp waking up which might be heard inside the tent by the aid-workers. The teacher/leader in the role of the camp co-ordinator arrives to brief the volunteers. She brings with her two boxes containing food and medical supplies for the volunteers' own use and tells them that there is enough food in the camp for the present number of refugees, but that there is absolutely no room for more; bringing new groups and families in will endanger the survival of those already in the camp. The dilemma that will face the volunteers is obvious and is fully discussed with the group before the action is resumed. The co-ordinator leaves to go to other camps in the area.

The volunteers make their first inspection of the camp; the rest of the group are asked by the teacher/leader not to take on the roles of the refugees but instead to adopt the physical positions of refugees, based on the images they have received from the media. The volunteers walk amongst the figures describing what they can see. The teacher/leader introduces a new role into the drama by narrating the idea of a figure sitting above the camp watching; he is a young prince sent out by his people to find help, he has walked for four nights and the people he has left behind depend on his influence to save them from death. As the prince approaches the tent the rest of the group can question him about his motives and hopes. He enters the tent and the volunteers have to deal with the dilemma he poses. Will they risk stretching the supplies? Can they face the prince with their own boxes of supplies untouched in front of them? The prince offers them his gold buckle and to work by carrying the boxes of supplies. The volunteers are able to go back to the groups that created the characters for further advice.

An initial concern to deal with the magnitude of the theme has been crystallized into the dilemma facing the volunteers; the dilemma leads to a consideration of what aid is, what real sharing of global resources might mean, and the tokenism of relieving guilt through giving to charity.

Experimenting with the use of conventions and the roles of actor and spectator allows the group to control a subtle and gradual shift from the real to the symbolic. For example, action can grow from the group using furniture and other objects to represent the place where they imagine the drama is taking place and from them talking about the space, its atmosphere and what is in it. Figures can be placed in the space to represent where characters might be at a particular moment in the drama—conversation about placing the figures will start the process of theatre-action for the group. The group can suggest motives, thoughts and words for the figures, as themselves or symbolically through conventions such as **Voices in the Head** or **Thought-tracking**. As interest grows in the context, the group may feel ready to enter the scene and interact together. But even if they do not, they have already begun to engage with theatre whilst appearing only to be commenting on the way in which they have visualized the scene of the drama.

Intentions for the Work

A further consideration in the matching process is the short- and long-term intentions of the work; the purposes underlying the group's use of theatre. The historic functions of theatre as an educative medium demonstrate that it is used in a variety of contexts which, briefly summarized, stretch from the psycho-therapeutic through documentary, satiric and didactic to cathartic entertainment. In educational contexts there is evidence that theatre is used for a wide range of purposes—often as part of a structured developmental programme that organizes learning purposes in the form of a syllabus to be followed, or as programmes of study leading to specific attainment targets. In common with other art-forms, both the long- and short-term educational objectives for theatre work can be classified within a compass-type model which has four points of reference:

● **Instrumental objectives**
  Specific, measurable goals relating to skill-development, conceptual development and knowledge.

● **Expressive objectives**
  Unspecific, indeterminate goals relating to the student's development of attitudes and values which may, or may not, occur through involvement in the dramatic action.

● **Aesthetic learning**
  Skills, concepts and knowledge relating to the art-form.

● **Personal and social learning**
  Skills, concepts and knowledge relating to self and the 'self/others' areas of learning provided in both the symbolic and real dimensions of the drama.

Categories of Action

It is important to consider the category of action best suited to the issue which is to become the focus of the drama:

Figure   3

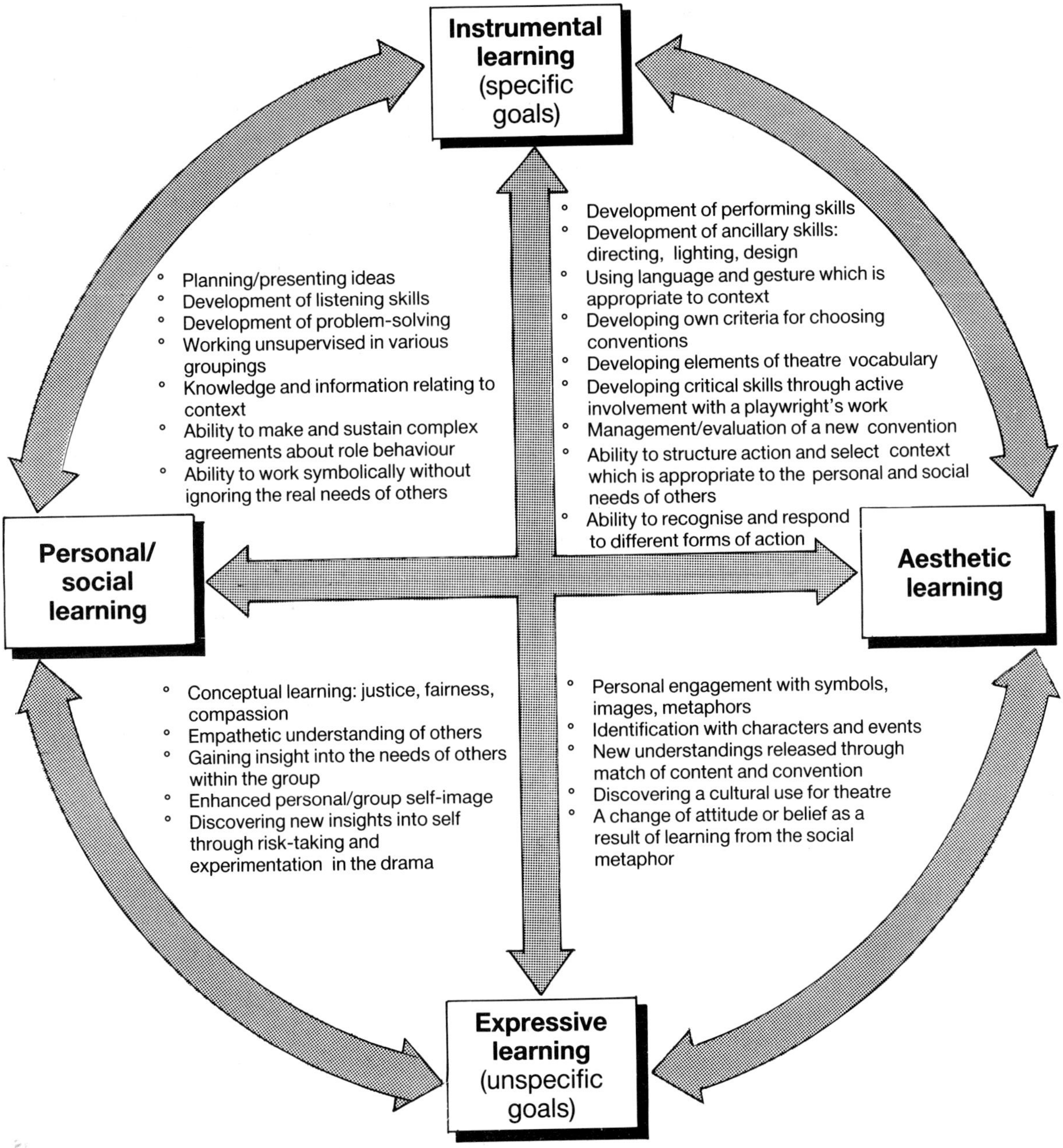

Instrumental learning (specific goals)

- ° Development of performing skills
- ° Development of ancillary skills: directing, lighting, design
- ° Using language and gesture which is appropriate to context
- ° Developing own criteria for choosing conventions
- ° Developing elements of theatre vocabulary
- ° Developing critical skills through active involvement with a playwright's work
- ° Management/evaluation of a new convention
- ° Ability to structure action and select context which is appropriate to the personal and social needs of others
- ° Ability to recognise and respond to different forms of action

- ° Planning/presenting ideas
- ° Development of listening skills
- ° Development of problem-solving
- ° Working unsupervised in various groupings
- ° Knowledge and information relating to context
- ° Ability to make and sustain complex agreements about role behaviour
- ° Ability to work symbolically without ignoring the real needs of others

Personal/ social learning

Aesthetic learning

- ° Conceptual learning: justice, fairness, compassion
- ° Empathetic understanding of others
- ° Gaining insight into the needs of others within the group
- ° Enhanced personal/group self-image
- ° Discovering new insights into self through risk-taking and experimentation in the drama

- ° Personal engagement with symbols, images, metaphors
- ° Identification with characters and events
- ° New understandings released through match of content and convention
- ° Discovering a cultural use for theatre
- ° A change of attitude or belief as a result of learning from the social metaphor

Expressive learning (unspecific goals)

○ **Context-building**

Does the space need re-arranging to represent the context for the action physically? Do characters need creating or fleshing out? Is any additional contextual information necessary?

◇ **Narrative**

Is there a need to clarify the story or to move it on through action? Will narrative action breed commitment to the drama through the strength of the story-line?

▽ **Poetic**

Do the group need to concentrate on making and communicating the symbols and images which represent their responses to the drama?

□ **Reflective**

Are things moving too quickly? Is there a need for action which requires consideration and thought? Is there a need for clarifying responses through the action?

Within each category, a further set of choices is available according to whether a direct or indirect form of entry is appropriate and what balance of spectators/actors is required either by the content or by the group. *Part One provides detailed information about the conventions within each category according to their uses and the level of demand made on participants, in order to assist in making a choice of convention at this level.*

Understanding the demands and functions of the conventions described in Part One gives the group and the teacher/leader the opportunity to make a match of convention to content which reflects the factors outlined above. The conventions offer a multiplicity of routes into the material. As an illustration, the list of ideas presented below gives an indication of some of the possibilities of matching convention to content for a group using theatre as a way of exploring a short story.

The challenge, and the satisfaction, for the teacher/leader lies in the level of creativity required to establish a priority order for the factors which will determine the appropriate match of convention to content for a group at a particular stage of its personal, social and aesthetic development.

Possible uses of theatre conventions as a means of deepening responses to a short story

Narrative action

Story conventions
—story told from different points of view;
—incidents talked about between pairs of characters;
—people outside the story commenting on the characters and events
  e.g. teachers, neighbours, social workers, relatives, etc.;
—scenes representing group prediction of next part of the story;
—telephone conversations in which one character tells another what's
  been happening.

Role-play conventions
—hot-seating characters about their motives and reactions;
—alternative scenes involving the characters;
—forum-theatre looking at alternative courses of action to those
described
  in the story;
—outline of character put up on wall and 'role' built during the reading of
  the story;
—teacher/leader in the role of one of the characters as a starting point, or
  interviewed by the class;
—meetings of characters e.g. the villagers, parish council, etc. chaired by
  the teacher or member of the class;
—'outside' broadcasts, news stories, chat shows involving characters or
  events from the story.

Context-building action

Still-Image conventions
—tableaux representing 'illustrations' to key events;
—family, or group, photographs—possibly contrasting public formal
  photos with private intimate photos;
—tableaux representing a character's image of events in the past or
future;
—freeze-frame convention from video as a way of holding action.

Physical-context conventions
—letters, diaries or notes written by, or between, characters;
—precious or important objects drawn or made by class;
—designing or drawing costumes;
—classroom re-arranged to represent an important 'space' e.g. a room, a
  cabin, or some other environment described in the book;
—compiling oral reports, dossiers, records, secret files kept by the
  security forces, police, etc.

3. Focus—learning through discovery and imagined experience

(see also *4. Theatre structure—generating meanings*, p. 65)

As the work progresses, the student's awareness of the content area will develop and change as a result of her responses to the 'here-and-now' experience provided through the action of the convention. Contextual atmosphere is created, symbols and images emerge, the student speaks and walks as another person and works with friends who are also projecting fictional roles. *It happens in all forms of theatre that the live experience of acting and spectating in itself begins the transformation of understandings about the area of experience that is represented in the drama.* It has already been suggested in this book that one of the unique qualities of theatre, as an arts medium, is that it is live, shared and subjectively experienced through its special uses and variations of time, space and presence. Until the work starts an artist, in any medium, is unlikely to have a clear idea of what a new piece of work should communicate or represent. She wants to discover her intentions through pitching her own individuality together with the ambiguities, dilemmas and mysteries suggested by an outline idea, or expression, through the craft of her art-form or chosen material.

If groups involved in theatre are to gain practical experience as artists, rather than spend their time as students learning about artists, then the teacher/leader needs to allow the focus for the work to emerge through the work and through the choices that the students take about the course of their work. *To be too definite and clear about the intentions and focus of the work in advance is to deny students the power and experience of being artists.*

Certain educational contexts make it difficult for teachers, in particular, to work in this way. Institutional contexts which promote a climate of accountability based on the delivery of measurable, pre-determined set tasks in pursuit of set goals press the teacher using theatre towards expressing only the instrumental features of their work at the expense of the vital, but indeterminate, expressive features.

4. Reflection—time out

(See also *Principles for Structuring Theatre for Learning Opportunities*, p. 60)

As artists progress they tend to take time away from their work in order to consider its development and what is being discovered as a result of working on the material. This reflection involves skills of perception, forming hypotheses, considering the tools and methods available and deciding on the next action before moving back to the work. *The reflective activity of the artist is likely to focus on the duality of the convention to content relationship; in other words, ideas about the content grow alongside ideas about how the medium or chosen material can be used to shape and communicate meanings.*

The Rosa Parks illustration that follows attempts to capture the quality of reflection brought about within a group who struggle to find the appropriate match between content and convention. It is a fitting conclusion to the view held in this book of theatre as a means of opening up and linking inner and outer worlds of experience.

Example 2— Realizing the intentions of the work

A group are exploring the role of social protest in a democratic society by examining the lives of 'ordinary' people whose protests were joined by others and led to social change e.g. Gandhi, Benny Rothman (Kinder Scout Trespass) and Rosa Parkes (the Alabama Bus Boycott). The work on Rosa Parkes comes from a source-story that describes the day she left work in a clothing factory, caught a racially segregated bus and refused to give up her seat to a white man when there were no white seats left on the bus. She was arrested and the incident led to the great bus boycott that gave birth to Martin Luther King's famous 'I have a dream . . .' speech.

The issue for the group's exploration through theatre lies in how to understand the pressures on Rosa at the point when she refused. Why did it happen that day? The group decide to construct the bus; the teacher/ leader suggests they find a way of building the bus to give it more dramatic potential than a naturally accurate bus. The bus enables the passengers to be seated facing others as well as in rows.

The group spent some time using a number of conventions in order to find the experience of being on the bus on that day. They try using a series of **Still-Images** to represent changing expressions and responses throughout the bus at key moments leading up to the refusal, they use **Thought-Tracking** on the passengers. They feel that this attempt to use poetic action is preventing them experiencing the action; pairs work on **Overheard Conversations** as well as a **Whole-Group Role-Play** with the volunteer playing Rosa trying to use **Teacher-in-Role** as a way of drawing the other passengers into the drama and probing differences of opinion amongst them as to what is happening. The group are still dissatisfied with their efforts, and feel that the role-play had shown that the cultural and historical differences between their lives and the lives of the Afro-American people on board the bus were too great. This leads to the reflection that Rosa's refusal was to do with the pain of her people's history as much as to do with events that day.

The group's discussion of the limitations of the conventions they have been using and the way in which their thinking is beginning to change and grow, suggests an idea to the teacher/leader to which the group agree. She asks the group to deconstruct the bus so that all that is left is Rosa seated and the white passenger and arresting officer standing next to her at the point of her last refusal to give up the seat. The group are asked to take their own time in joining a group image, built around Rosa, which represents the images in Rosa's mind at that moment when she decided to refuse. All those in the group who choose to contribute join the **Still-Image** which reflects slavery, injustice, prejudice, anger and fear. As the teacher watches and is affected by the power of the symbols in the image, as well as by the atmosphere the image was creating, the next question is formed: 'Think of other times, throughout history, when black people have travelled in the white man's transport ... What are the words and sounds that come back across history to remind us of those experiences?'. The combination of the **Soundtracking**, together with the image of Rosa, the passenger and the police surrounded by other powerful images made by the rest of the group, is very moving. Poetic action had been used to overcome problems experienced in previous attempts made through context-building action and narrative action. The power of the symbols and atmosphere together with the tension of form help the group to break through their block and see the purpose of the drama on a historic and universal scale.

Having identified the historic link through the poetic action, the group feel that they are better equipped to manage narrative action in the form of a **Whole-Group Role-Play** at Rosa's workplace the morning after the incident. The group manage the role-play so that they can improvise the relationships between different groups of workers: black machinists/ white machinists; overseers and managers; white cleaning staff who are paid less than the machinists like Rosa and the company boss.